EXPERIENCE OF PARENTS
IN SEEKING TREATMENT FOR
THEIR CHILD DIAGNOSED WITH
ADHD

by

Tenise M. Wall, Ph.D.

Author: Tenise M. Wall, Ph.D. New York
Publisher: DBC Publishing, Virginia Beach / Richmond, VA

Copyright ©   2016
ISBN Numbers   ISBN-13: 978-0692825655
                     ISBN-10: 0692825657

Follow the author on social media or contact her via:

Web-site: www.drwall2016.com
Linked In: www.linkedin.com/in/tenisewall
Facebook: https://www.facebook.com/drwall2016/
E-mail: drwall2016@yahoo.com

Table of Contents

EXPERIENCE OF PARENTS IN SEEKING TREATMENT FOR THEIR CHILD DIAGNOSED WITH ATTENTION DEFICIT HYPERACTIVITY DISORDER

By

Tenise M. Wall, Ph.D.

Marial Martyn, PhD, Faculty Mentor and Chair

Steven Schneider, PhD, Committee Member

Antonio Santonastasi, PhD, Committee Member

Andrea Miller, PhD, Dean of Psychology

Harold Abel School of Social and Behavioral Sciences

A Dissertation Presented in Partial Fulfillment
of the Requirements for the Degree of
Doctor of Philosophy

Capella University
May 2016

Abstract

Attention deficit hyperactivity disorder (ADHD) continues to be a prevalent childhood diagnosis, for which parents seek treatment for their children. The purpose of the study was to examine the experiences of parents as they seek treatment for their child diagnosed with ADHD. This qualitative case study used Yin's theoretical framework and included participants from one county in a Northeastern state of the United States. The participants consisted of 10 Caucasian mothers, who have a child between the ages of 5-18 years old whom has been diagnosed by a medical professional with ADHD. The data was gathered through conversational style interviews containing open-ended questions. The data was analyzed using a line-by-line and cross-case data analysis, following Yin's model.

Results of this study showed persistent challenges parents faced with school systems. Many participants felt schools were the most difficult part of their treatment seeking experiences, and reported frustration about not having 504 Accommodations implemented, or resources provided. Both Barkley's theory and parental motivation theory were evident in these school findings.

Participants expressed the challenge of not having community resources available to them, or their child, which increased the sense of isolation, and supported social stigma theory. Future recommendations involve providing teachers with comprehensive education on the etiology and evidenced-based, best practices for working with children with ADHD.

The implications for social change include practitioners, schools, and the medical community increasing their understanding of parental treatment seeking experiences, and address such barriers, to enhance treatment services.

Dedication & Acknowledgments

This dissertation is dedicated to one other person (besides my husband) who pushed me harder, supported me fully, encouraged me, and believed in me completely; my step-mother, or as I like to refer to her, my second mother Karen (Kay) McGee. Kay was a woman of great faith, wisdom, strength, and she would tell you like it is whether you hear or forbear, but all in love. She was small in stature, but big in power of the impact she had in people's lives. As I embarked on this dissertation journey, Kay became one of my biggest supporters, who pushed me like a coach of a boxer who is in the ring of life. Her words often echoed in my ears, "Everything was possible," because it was all inside of me. On December 23, 2015, Kay went home to be with the Lord, but her spirit of strength, faith, and tenacity echoed for me to keep pushing forward, "You're going to do it!" Kay had every intention on being at my Doctoral graduation and our last conversation involved that topic. I told Kay, depending on when I finished, the graduation would be in New Orleans or Minneapolis. Kay remarked "Well you better get on it, because I don't want to go to Minneapolis." We laughed and continued talking. My graduation was set for Minneapolis. I knew Kay was right there watching over us, cheering me on, saying, "See I told you, you could do it," even if she preferred New Orleans. To my forever angel, I'll love you forever Kay, rest in God's peace.

I would like to acknowledge my Lord and Savior, Jesus Christ, who I have drawn my strength and faith from in completing this dissertation journey. That faith has allowed me to continue despite the challenges that arose along the way. When I felt overwhelmed I prayed, when I thought I would never make it through a half a dozen statistics courses, I prayed, when I lost three family members and one dear friend who passed away, I prayed, and He kept me through it all.

I acknowledge my husband, Troy D. Wall, who has been my rock and greatest supporter. He is the one who maintained the home front when I spent countless hours every week studying, researching, reading, and writing. He cooked meals, maintained the home, transported kids, and was there providing loving words of encouragement, "You can do it!" The sacrifice of time, resources, and energy was not of my own, but of our family, and I thank him for that dearly. He was my driver, taking me to colloquiums in Florida, Georgia, and Virginia. Our summer vacations during those years were built around Capella requirements and he never complained. Instead he cared for the kids during the day while I attended classes, then picked me up, and ensured my needs. When I accept my degree, it is not just my own, but ours. I love you forever, Babe!

Before ever being assigned a dissertation mentor, my husband and I prayed for mine. We prayed they would be knowledgeable, supportive, and responsive to my needs. I believe my prayers were answered with Dr. Marial Martyn, PhD. When I enrolled at Capella, I asked how long does the dissertation process take? They told me it depends on the learner. The least amount of time was one and a half years, but that meant a lot of work on the part of the learner, they said. Once I heard that, it became my personal goal to complete my own dissertation in that time frame. There is no way I would have been able to move along the dissertation course without the support I had from Dr. Martyn. She was responsive to the questions I had, knowledgeable about the qualitative methodology, provided prompt, clear feedback, and availed herself by e-mail and phone. She was an absolute Godsend, and I appreciate her commitment to her work very much.

My committee members: Dr. Steven Schneider, PhD, and Dr. Antonio Santonastasi, PhD were excellent to work with as they provided prompt feedback and were committed in seeing me move forward.

Pastor Pierre Berard came into our lives at just the right time and season, and assisted us in ways that cannot be outlined here. He knows, and we know, how God used him to be a tremendous blessing in our lives and to help in ways others refused. My husband and I have made a life-long friend connected through this dissertation journey.

I am so thankful to the parents who agreed to participate in this research study. They opened their lives to me during those interviews, shared their triumphs, struggles and pain, and allowed me a greater understanding of what they experienced. They all were so helpful, and many concluded stating they hoped their interview helped me. Since I cannot acknowledge them by name, I give them a collective shout of praise; Thank you! You have helped the research community tremendously!

I have many family members and friends whom offered their support through encouraging words, checking in on the process and believing in me. That often fueled the flame to keep moving forward. My youngest of three children, Alexis Wall, played a special role in all of this considering five of the nine years of her life, I have been working on this degree. She learned to understand why Mommy was always stuck at a computer, while at the same time she was my reason to 'stop and smell the roses.' When I celebrated a milestone, she was there to congratulate me, and when I got closer to the end she was there to praise me, "Good job Mama!"

For me, this journey has been about breaking barriers and refuting statistics. I was a teenage mother who became a single mother of two for many years before meeting my husband. I was told by a man whose job was to determine if I could get access to childcare funds to return to school for my Associate's degree, who told me my goal was unrealistic. He denied access to a childcare program, because he did not believe I could obtain an Associate's degree. I went back to college anyway and earned an Associate's degree in 2001, a Bachelors in 2002, a Masters in 2003, and here we are now in 2016; Dr. Tenise M. Wall, PhD, LMSW, CASAC-T. And with that I say, to God be the glory! Never let anyone define who you are and dictate what you can become. If you can conceive it, and you believe it, then you will achieve it. To all my fellow doctoral cohorts, I leave you with this, keep pressing forward!

Tenise M. Wall

CHAPTER 1. INTRODUCTION

Background of the Problem

Attention Deficit Hyperactivity Disorder (ADHD) is a childhood disorder which has been studied from various aspects. The background for this study is to understand the experiences of parents whose children have been diagnosed with ADHD. This research further probed parental experiences in seeking outpatient mental health, medication, and intervention treatment services for their children. Children and adolescents with ADHD often struggle academically, socially, and behaviorally in the school setting. In the school setting educators often do not understand the disorder and can become frustrated with what they perceive is the parents' lack of control over their child's behaviors (Mills, 2011). As a parent perceives this frustration, they can become defensive rather than building a trusting alliance with the school system. With misunderstandings, frustration, and/or criticism on either side, the one who suffers is the child (Mills, 2011). As practitioners consider parental preferences to treatment they directly impact the positive clinical outcomes, given that a parents' acceptance and support can directly impact outcomes (Fegert, Slawik, Wermelskirchen, Nübling, & Mühlbacher, 2011). It is pertinent to the field of mental health to understand the parental experience of pursuing therapeutic interventions for their children diagnosed with ADHD, as more children meet the diagnostic criteria for the disorder. It is also necessary to understand any challenges and barriers met by parents to intervention services. The proposed research question related to the background of this study as it focused on identifying key attributes of the parental experience.

Bussing, Zima, Gary, and Wilson-Garvan (2003) discussed the need to explicate in the research literature the experience of seeking services for ADHD treatment. In their study, they found significant differences in gender and race/ethnicity variations and suggested future research to probe contributing factors prompting parents to seek treatment (Bussing et al., 2003). In one study where the decision-making processes were compared amongst parents who chose to medicate their child with ADHD and those who chose not to, they found no significant differences between the two (Mills, 2011). Mills (2011) stated that becoming better informed in that matter could lead to improved communication and treatment planning while strengthening the professional relationship, and trust. This topic is important, given that parental factors are the key determinant of services usage (Sayal, Ford, & Goodman, 2010). In the research performed by Sayal et al. (2010) the researchers examined changes in rates and correlating factors for children diagnosed with ADHD. They found that despite most parents recognizing there was a problem; more than half felt it was hyperactivity and the greatest determinant appeared to be when there was the presence of a comorbidity of emotional or behavioral disorders (Sayal et al., 2010). The relevance of this study to the proposed research is acknowledging the key role parents have in determining treatment for their child. It also remarks about the effects of childhood ADHD left untreated which often continues into adolescence and adulthood with significant adverse outcomes: other psychiatric, impaired academics, and social attainment (Sayal et al., 2010). This dissertation advanced the scientific knowledge on this topic as findings presented insightful information to a parent's experience as they sought treatment for their child diagnosed with ADHD. Understanding the nuances, challenges, and successes in the experience of seeking treatment has a direct impact on treatment obtainment and acceptance (Charach, Yeung, Volpe, Goodale, & dosReis, 2014).

In the research performed by Sayal et al. (2010) the researchers examined changes in rates and correlating factors for children diagnosed with ADHD. The research took place in Britain and examined both the recognition of ADHD by the medical community along with factors associated with parents seeking treatment. It was found that Britain had much lower rates of ADHD prevalence which could be attributed to the stringent guidelines practitioners used in diagnosing the disorder (Sayal et al., 2010). American practitioners were often found to diagnosis when hyperactivity or inattention was present but British practitioners often only diagnosed for ADHD when both symptoms were manifested

(Sayal et al., 2010). The authors found there was a sharp increase in parental awareness of ADHD over the course of their study and correlated this increased awareness with increased service use. They found that despite most parents recognizing there was a problem; more than half felt it was hyperactivity. The greatest determinant to pursuing treatment appeared to be when there was the presence of a comorbidity of emotional or behavioral disorder (Sayal et al., 2010). This study supports the key role parents have in determining treatment for their child. Improved parental awareness has the potential to impact the connection between children and ADHD services. Some of the correlations between seeking treatment and parental experience was the parental awareness of the ADHD disorder.

In the article by Ahmed, Hons, McCaffery, and Aslani (2013) the authors discussed the influential factors of parents as they determine to use medication as a form of treatment for their child with ADHD. The authors used a systematic review process. They obtained eleven research studies within their final data to review the factors contributing to the parent's decision to pursue stimulant medication treatment. Some of the prevalence rates noted were 50% of childhood ADHD that continues into adolescence and 30% - 60% continuing from those numbers into adulthood (Ahmed et al., 2013). The four main themes that evolved from the research were confronting the diagnosis, external influences, apprehension regarding stimulant medication treatment, and experiences with the healthcare system (Ahmed et al., 2013). The authors were able to deconstruct the main themes of their study. It is a crucial role of healthcare providers to understand the factors that influence a parent's decision making when choosing a stimulant medication treatment or other. Such external factors and experiences of the healthcare system call for further examination.

The role of parents continues to be the primary factor whether a child accepts a medication therapy to assist in treating ADHD (Charach, Yeung, Volpe, Goodale, & dosReis, 2014). In the article by Charach et al. (2014) they examined the use of stimulant treatment and perspectives of parents and young adults. Beliefs about the diagnosis of ADHD and the use of medication as an intervention strategy were probed and outlined in the study. A separate section was provided for the process of deciding whether to use medication as a treatment source for the ADHD diagnosis. The parental beliefs about ADHD for a majority of the participants was that it is a medical illness requiring treatment. Another belief contended it was a physical condition whereby some treatment or accommodation was needed (Charach et al., 2014). The author found a greater disparity in the beliefs of the young adults than their parent counterparts. While parents have almost complete control over the treatment decisions for young children there is a shift that begins to occur as children age. Young adults play a greater role in the decision-making process and when and how to bring them into the discussion should be carefully managed by the healthcare provider. The young person's beliefs and attitudes are often predictors of medication continuity. Parents maintain a significant role in shaping the beliefs and attitudes of ADHD and treatment measures in the lives and minds of their children (Charach et al., 2014).

The literature review found a number of articles pertaining to the parental experience of the decision-making process of stimulant medication. In the articles presented here there were various themes presented for parents as they pondered the decision to medicate their child for ADHD symptoms. The determining factor often was associated with a parent's beliefs and attitudes towards the diagnosis of ADHD and the use of medication as a source to control the symptoms. The research proposed differed in that it examined the overall experience of the parent as they pursued treatment rather than focused on their experience with one form of treatment. The topic of parental experience in seeking treatment is important, given that parental factors are the key determinant of services usage (Sayal et al., 2010).

Statement of the Problem

The specific topic studied was the parents' experience of seeking treatment for their children. Parents of children between the ages of 5 to 18 years who had been diagnosed with ADHD was the focus of this study. An exploration of their engagement in outpatient mental health services and various intervention treatment options were probed. Parents determine if their child receives ADHD treatment services or not. Despite this fact, parental experience of seeking treatment is an area that has not been widely studied (Johnston et al., 2005). There can be many factors that contribute to a parent's decision such as issues connected to etiological attributions, to life events instead of genetics, the perception that the behavior is not significant, or the belief that the duration of the time course will be minimal (Bussing et al., 2003).

The selected topic, parental experience of pursuing ADHD treatment for their children, related to the field of psychology by exploring a common childhood disorder (Peters & Jackson, 2009). When children receive treatment from practitioners in relation to the symptoms manifested by ADHD, psychologists are often among those servicing such clients. Parenting support and psycho education, along with counseling, and behavioral skills are often accessed in the therapist's office. Psychologists have the ability to provide services to the individual child or family system, and it is imperative for practitioners to have a clear understanding when treatment recommendations are not obtained.

Purpose of the Study

The purpose of this study was to explore the
various experiences parents had as they sought
treatment services for their children diagnosed with
ADHD. Often there are challenges and/or barriers in
treatment seeking which impact a parent's ability to
follow through with treatment recommendations.
Understanding such challenges and/or barriers to
treatment seeking was also beneficial in examining
the overall parental experience. The information
uncovered in the research can improve
communication between parents and practitioners
while strengthening relationships and trust and
improving treatment planning (Mills, 2011). Given the
discrepancies in messages a parent may receive
concerning ADHD from medical practitioners,
journalists, and politicians which could be
diametrically opposed, the hesitancy parents have in
pursuing treatment is understandable (Taylor,
O'Donoghue, & Houghton, 2006).

The methods used in this study were able to
answer the research question by allowing the
participants the ability to extend their responses

through open ended questions. The semi-structured approach guided participants in an over-arching area but the specifics of what they conveyed were based on their personal experiences and what they found relevant. This approach captured the parental nuisances' specific to their experience in seeking treatment. There are studies that examine a parents' experience in using a particular modality to treat ADHD, predominantly the use of stimulant medication, however the examination of the overall experience took what had been studied and looked at it in a different perspective (Hamrin, McCarthy, & Tyson, 2010; Stroh, Frankenberger, Cornell-Swanson, Wood & Pahl, 2008; Taylor, O'Donoghue, & Houghton, 2006). It broadened the scope of the investigation to capture the challenges that arose from seeking treatment in general instead of seeking a particular type of ADHD treatment.

Significance of the Study

This study provides useful information for the medical doctors and mental health practitioners who work with families to understand the parental experiences of seeking treatment for their children with ADHD. Mychailszyn, DosReis, and Myers (2008) stated some of the benefits of the findings of such research would include the successful engagement with clinicians who recognize how parents understand their child and the presenting issues which they have sought treatment. Parents could understand implications for them, their child, and their family, and what such a diagnosis can have on them. Some studies have remarked about the effects of childhood ADHD left untreated which often continues into adolescence and adulthood with significant adverse outcomes: other psychiatric disorders, impaired academics, and social attainment (Sayal et al., 2010). Further research regarding parental experience can allow for better access to optimal care, hope for future research, and better education for families (Hervey-Jumper et al., 2006). The more a practitioner knows about the trends and commonly held beliefs of parents the better they may be in their attempts to engage parent participation in the treatment plan (Olaniyan et al., 2007).

ADHD treatment relates to the specialization area of this researcher- General Psychology. The General Psychology specialization covers a multitude of topics from micro- to macro-level and individuals to families and groups. Unlike other specializations that focus on one specific area of psychological study, General Psychology allows the researcher to use their research focused skills to probe many areas which would include ADHD and parents. The inquiry of the topic of ADHD is related to both the field of psychology and the specialization of this researcher.

The research study provides a description of the parental experience of seeking treatment for their children diagnosed with ADHD. This study sought to explore the experiences of parents as they navigated systems to pursue ADHD treatment. It is important for practitioners to understand how parents perceive treatment for ADHD as optimal clinical outcomes are based on the shared decision making and agreement between all parties, to include parents, children, psychologists, social workers, teachers, physicians, and other collaterals (Fegert et al., 2011). A potential psychological lesson developed by this study is be the ability to inform practitioners; assisting in the development of their treatment recommendations.

Research Design

Methodology

The research methodology used for this research study was qualitative with the use of a case study approach. Yin (2009) describes the single- and multiple-case study designs. The single-case can be used when there is an inquiry of an individual, a school, or an organization. A multiple-case study would examine the phenomenon among several individuals, schools, or organizations (Yin, 2009). This research study employed a multiple-case study. The use of multiple parents as participants rather than one parent as a critical case is what made this a multiple-case design. The three types of case studies presented by Yin (2009) are exploratory, descriptive, and explanatory. This study described the experiences of parents seeking treatment in a descriptive case study. Case study research has six sources of evidence used by researchers that consist of documentation, archival records, interviews, direct observations, participant-observations, and physical artifacts (Yin, 2009). The participant interviews were an essential piece of data collection, that focused the questions on the phenomenon of parental experience of seeking treatment for their children who are diagnosed with ADHD. This was an opportunity to gain insight into the direct parental experiential factors. Additionally, direct observations of participants were made during the interview process, and any documentation parents wanted to share with this researcher, relevant to their child's ADHD diagnosis and experiences, were reviewed. A case study uses a much smaller participant range than that of a quantitative methodology. Because of the lower participant range, the findings are not easily generalizable as is the case with quantitative studies. Despite challenges in generalizing findings, the case study does have great value to the research community. Case studies allow for an in-depth look at a specific phenomenon that would not be allowable with the large numbers of participants used in quantitative work.

Sample Selection

The larger population from which the sample was drawn were adult men and women who were parents of a child who had been diagnosed with ADHD. The sample was biological parents of such diagnosed children. Parents were either a mother or father. The sample must have sought treatment services for their child's ADHD symptoms. The sample size was 8-14 participants or until saturation was met. Although Yin (2009) does not provide an exact sample size, he does state that obtaining certainty in one's findings would correlate with an increased number of replications within ones' study, containing five, six, or more of such replications.

The type of sampling strategy used was purposeful sampling. More specifically purposeful sampling was used to obtain research participants. Purposeful sampling allowed this researcher to use the participants who were available during the time the data was collected. The essence of purposeful samples is the accessibility between the researcher and potential research participants (Marshall, 1996).

The sampling strategy consisted of recruiting
participants through community networks through
local churches. Contact was made with religious
leaders of local churches to request their assistance
in disseminating the information about the research
study. This information was read with the church's
announcements during service, flyers were posted on
bulletin boards, and/or this researcher shared the
information directly with the congregation when given
the opportunity. All information encouraged the reader
to share the information with those who may qualify
for inclusion in the research study. Interested
participants made contact by calling the phone
number listed on the informational items, such as
flyers. Once participants contacted this researcher to
inquire about participating they were screened for
several items. An initial telephone screening was
used to ascertain the appropriateness of those parties
interested in participating. The first step was to
confirm they were the biological parent of the child
and secondly that their child had received a diagnosis
from a medical professional. The children were
between the ages of 5 and 18 and lived at home with
their parents. Following the screening, those parents

who meet the criteria were asked to sign written consent giving their permission to participate in the study. After written consent was provided a day and time was scheduled for the interview to be performed.

Data Collection Methods

The interview began following the preliminaries, and the data was collected through semi-structured interviews utilizing open-ended questions designed by this learner. The questions were asked in a free-flowing manner which resembled more of an informal conversation than a rigid question-response experience. Interviews were approximately 60-90 minutes in duration. Once the interview questions were completed and the participant was asked to offer any additional comments or feedback that had not been asked, the session was concluded. The participants were thanked for their participation in this research study. Participants were informed they may be contacted as the data was analyzed for checking information and/or meaning of interview content. Participants received a $20 gift card for their participation in this study. There were field notes taken after each session as needed.

Following the interview, both the audio recordings and field notes were later transcribed verbatim. The audio recordings and field notes were transcribed by this researcher. The participants were coded as Participant 1, Participant 2, etc. The data was backed up in several places and lastly, secured. The data: original audiotapes and original transcription were kept in a lockbox at a financial institution. Field notes were also typed, organized, saved, scanned into a computer, and managed in the same fashion as the audiotapes and transcriptions.

Data Analysis Methods

The first step in the data analysis was the preparation of the data which began by transcribing verbatim the participants' interviews. Interviews were transcribed by this researcher. Once the transcriptions were complete they went through the next step of data reduction using qualitative data analysis software, NVivo. Once the software provided the output, this researcher then worked through the data and examined all pertinent categories of data and the emergence of patterns and meaningful occurrences (Yin, 2009). As such categories were further reviewed; the emergence of themes were noted and supported by the content of the interviews. This portion of the data analysis continued with the probing of each case. Once each case had gone through this process of inquiry, the use of cross-case synthesis was incorporated. This process allowed for integrating meaning across cases. The use of a word table- displaying data from each case was helpful. This cross-case synthesis brought meaning to multiple-cases and prompted the interpretation of such synthesis by this researcher. The Hierarchical analysis continued to break down the main themes into sub-themes. Once the data analysis software categorized the data, this researcher further looked at the data's patterns and themes and reduced further as needed. In concluding with the data analysis, data was probed for similarities and differences in both a case analysis perspective and cross case analysis, and therefore generalizations were made regarding overall parental experiences in seeking treatment.

Data Presentation Methods

NVivo software was used in categorization of items that assisted this researcher in the ability to analyze the data in a more efficient manner. Word tables displaying the data from each parent (case) was created with a uniform framework (Yin, 2009). There were additional word tables created to reflect various outcomes of interest and processes allowing for cross-case conclusions to be drawn (Yin, 2009). A cross-case synthesis was applied given there were multiple-cases being analyzed. In this final step of conclusions and verification of the data, it was important to examine any possible researcher bias from assumptions to conclusions. One way this was accomplished was through triangulation. Triangulation of data was used using interview observations, the interview itself, questionnaires, and any documents provided by the participants. Further verification of data incorporated member checking what the information obtained and/or the interpretation of the data was discussed and clarified with participants ensuring the meaning was accurate. Each case was summarized pertaining to the content provided by the interviewing phase and demographic surveys provided to each participant. The interpretation of the research data was then compared/contrasted to the current research literature on the subject and connections were made. The general theme of parental experience in seeking treatment for their children with ADHD and interpretative conclusions illustrated the connection between categories. In summation, it was important for this researcher to attend to all the presenting evidence, consider all major rival interpretations, focus on the most significant aspects and use prior expert knowledge within the analysis phase (Yin, 2009).

Credibility

In any research, there is an expectation the work would uphold all ethical and clinical standards set forth by its field of study. In qualitative work there should be a concise effort to present trustworthy research; one which makes a concerted effort to present the research participants' perspectives accurately (Lietz & Zayas, 2010). Qualitative work invokes the terms: credibility, dependability, and transferability. Each term works in collaboration with the next to build a research study that is trustworthy to the professional literature.

There are several ways a researcher can build credibility within their research study, and one way is through triangulation. Triangulation can be done through the use of observer or data triangulation. Creswell (2013) describes triangulation as the use of multiple theoretical schemes, methods, or data sources. In this researcher's study, due to the use of a sole researcher, there was not observer triangulation, but there was data triangulation. The research plan consists of the collection of data from multiple sources, and was primarily made up of participant interviews. Member checking was another avenue to build credibility that this researcher utilized. One way, that member checking was performed following the transcribing of data, was to check with each participant for its accuracy. Upon completion of the data analysis, this researcher inquired with participants once again to ensure the analysis is reflective of their experiences.

Credibility speaks to the researchers' ability to present findings in an accurate manner representative of the participants' meanings (Lietz & Zayas, 2010). Research sessions attempted to reduce research reactivity by employing audiotapes that were discretely placed with advance knowledge of taping with the participant. As credibility was sought, many attempts to reduce researcher bias was enacted from discussing biases with mentor, seeking professional supervision as needed, increasing self-awareness, and keeping a written journal throughout the research process. Establishing credibility of this researcher was in presenting research findings which were true and accurate representations of the participants involved. The aforementioned measures confirmed this.

Transferability

Transferability was a key component to ensuring the research trustworthiness. In any research proposal, one is expected to state how their research findings contribute to the field of research in which they are seeking to embark. The various ways research can contribute to theory, expand the practice, and direct future research will all speak to a research's transferability (Lietz & Zayas, 2010). A thorough representation of the phenomenon of seeking treatment for children with ADHD, and its context perceived and experienced by the parents was presented (Lietz & Zayas, 2010). Another way to demonstrate the transferability was by showing the participants are knowledgeable about the topic being discussed and have the experiential knowledge to share such experiences to be beneficial to the psychological field of study. This was shown by selecting participants who best reflect the target population.

Dependability

Dependability was achieved in this research through measures from procedures and methods to descriptive information that can be reproduced by another researcher. This researcher incorporated rich and thick descriptions of the research, which allowed the readers to step into the participants' experiences (Creswell, 2013). In the article by Lietz and Zayas (2010) they use the term conformability to describe dependability where two meanings are intertwined. A negative case analysis is another vehicle to provide dependability at which time this researcher could have sought out a case with complexities and dilemmas and presented them openly assisting with intellectual honesty and political strategy (Patton, 2002). To ensure dependability this researcher utilized professional supervision, debriefings with assigned mentor and as previously stated member checking and audit trails (Lietz & Zayas, 2010). This researcher used an audit trail, which outlines the process and procedures of the research study along the way and includes documented reflexivity (Lietz & Zayas, 2010). This researcher used Google Docs within the proposed research study which allowed the ability to document and track research meetings, researcher decisions, and participant reactions following coding of transcripts (Lietz & Zayas, 2010).

This researcher's study as previously stated included reflexivity, peer debriefing, audit trails, prolonged engagement, triangulation, member checking and rich, thick descriptions. Including these aspects in this study increased the acceptability as a trustworthy research design and later findings.

Research Question

This research examined the parental experiences of seeking treatment for their children diagnosed with ADHD. The primary research question was explored: *What is the experience of parents in seeking treatment for their child who is diagnosed with attention deficit hyperactivity disorder?* Qualitative studies do not have hypotheses because they are not attempting to prove or disprove a theory but rather gain a deeper understanding of a phenomenon, from the examination of themes and patterns that evolve from the data (Yin, 2009).

Assumptions and Limitations

General Methodological Assumptions

The general methodological assumptions were that the use of a qualitative case study design obtained the rich and meaningful data often associated with this methodology (Yin, 2009). Case studies allow for the in-depth examination of a phenomenon (Yin, 2009). It was assumed inquiring into parental treatment seeking experiences using such method, would gather rich and detailed data of each participant's experience. It was assumed that although there would be similarities and differences among participants, their individual experiences would provide a depth of knowledge into each occurrence.

Theoretical Assumptions

The theoretical assumptions used to guide this research were Dr. Barkley's ADHD theory, parent motivation, and social stigma. Barkley's theory on ADHD integrated with executive function and self-regulation. Dr. Barkley's theory focused the diagnosis on a neurological basis and described it more of an issue of the inability to self-regulate than a disorder of behavior (Barkley, 2007). The executive function is the area most impacted in the pre-frontal lobe of the brain which causes deficits in a person's ability to regulate their emotions, affects non-verbal and verbal working memory, motivation, planning, problem-solving, response inhibitions, and goal-directed tasks (Barkley, 1997). Barkley's theory related to this dissertation study as it shaped the understanding of the ADHD diagnosis to a neurological deficit and could eventually influence the parental pursuit of ADHD treatment.

The second theoretical assumption was parent motivation. Parental motivation assumed parents' level of treatment engagement influenced their motivation. Motivation was assumed to be influenced by different variables, all of which impact parental treatment seeking experience (Bussing et al., 2007). The third theoretical assumption was social stigma. It was assumed that parents with children with ADHD did experience some level of stigma. Assumptions about social stigma were that parents were less likely to engage in treatment if they felt stigmatized; socially or internally (Mueller, Fuermaier, Koerts, & Tucha, 2012). Further assumptions were that stigma directed parental decisions whether to seek treatment and their subsequent experience with treatment providers and interventions (Mueller et al., 2012).

Topic Specific Assumptions

The topic of parental experience of seeking treatment for ADHD assumed parents who sought treatment had favorable or non-favorable experiences to share with this researcher allowing insight into what it was like for their family as they pursued interventions. It was also assumed there was some exchange between the school system and the parent during the earlier stages when treatment was prompted. This assumption was formed by accepting Dr. Barkley's theory on ADHD being a neurologically based disorder, impacting self-regulation and executive function. The literature also showed a high rate of comorbidity with ADHD and other disorders but in particular learning disabilities (Goldman et al., 1998). A school system would be one source to identify learning disabilities and therefore communicating such to the parent.

Assumptions About Instruments

Instruments used in research involve a number of assumptions. The use of interviews assumed participants would be expressing truthful accounts of their experience of treatment seeking. It was also assumed participants would be able to recall their experiences and verbally present them during a scheduled interview session. Further assumptions about the qualitative interviews were, they produced rich and meaningful data providing great insight into the parental experience (Yin, 2009).

Limitations

Although there are many benefits of conducting a qualitative study, one of the limitations in this study was the small sample size. Sample size can often be one of the limitations in qualitative work because it is difficult to generalize the results to larger populations (Yin, 2009). Another limitation of this study was the participants came from one county within one state. The findings in other counties or other states may be different based on factors that may make treatment seeking experiences different, such as accessibility to treatment, availability to ADHD information, school-based programs, or any number of factors. Lastly, the interview data depended upon the participants being honest, forthcoming, and having the ability to recall their experiences of seeking treatment.

Definition of Terms

ADHD. Attention deficit hyperactivity disorder (ADHD) is a diagnosis that is given by a qualified licensed practitioner following the strict guidelines as outlined in the *Diagnostic Statistical Manual 4.* To qualify under criterion "A" there must be a minimum of six inattentions and/or six hyperactivity/impulsivity symptoms that are manifested along with impairing symptoms occurring prior to the age of seven (Barzman, Fieler, & Sallee, 2004).

Parent. In this research, a parent constituted any biological mother or father who was the primary caregiver and had a child between the ages of five and 18 years of age who had been diagnosed with ADHD. Parents were of any age, race or ethnicity (Pham, Carlson, & Kosciulek, 2009).

Children. Children were defined as an individual who is school-age; between five and 18 years of age (Berger-Jenkins, McKay, Newcorn, Bannon, & Laraque, 2012). Children considered for the study were enrolled in school and had a diagnosis of ADHD confirmed by the parent. Children included males and females. Children demonstrated an array of symptomology prompting parents to seek intervention services such as poor academics, lack of behavioral control, inability to follow directions, conflictual familial relationships, emotional and self-esteem problems, and withdraw (dosReis, Mychailyszyn, Myers, & Riley, 2007).

Treatment options. Treatment options for children with ADHD can vary greatly from vitamin/naturopathic to the use of medication; which is the most commonly used treatment for ADHD. The treatments probed included but were not limited to the following: using behavior management, medication, vitamins, supplements, assistance in the educational setting, various therapeutic treatments to include individual, family and bio/neurological feedback treatment, or other (Johnston et al., 2005).

Expected Findings

Qualitative studies do not have expected findings as their goal is to gather meaning from the examination of a phenomenon such as the experience of parents seeking treatment for their children diagnosed with ADHD.

Researcher Biases for Consideration

The researcher expected findings were there was a deeper understanding of what a parent experiences as they sought treatment for their children diagnosed with ADHD. It was expected that patterns were presented in this qualitative study and common themes among participants were found.

The researcher's bias about this topic surrounded the interactions between the healthcare industry and parents seeking ADHD treatment. In working with parents of children diagnosed with ADHD in the role of a school social worker from 2004 -2015, some had reported they had not been treated adequately when they sought assistance. Although this had only been reported by a small group of parents, it was a factor this researcher was aware may have become a bias. One of the ways this was avoided in this research study was to share some of the preliminary findings with the assigned mentor and other colleagues who offered alternative explanations or further data collection may have been suggested

(Yin, 2009). Additionally, ongoing journaling was used as a method to reduce researcher bias.

This researcher is a Licensed Master Social Worker, who has extensive experience working with children with ADHD. Being employed as a school social worker from 2004-2015 has allowed for ongoing interactions with children and parents regarding such diagnosis. Furthermore, this researcher was a graduate student at Capella University with a major in General Psychology. Some of the coursework achieved through Capella University had included such courses as Qualitative Analysis and Advanced Qualitative Analysis. Additional learning experiences were through the research courses presented throughout the Track I, II, and III Capella Colloquiums. Throughout the process of data collection and analysis, the researcher returned to the data ensuring that interviews and data analysis were accurate representations of the meanings communicated by the participants. The researcher continued to become knowledgeable about the case study methodology by continued readings of research articles about case studies and those which have used case studies, dissertations having used case studies, and the Yin text. Furthermore, any personal matters, judgments, or experiences that came up which may have influenced the data analysis and interpretation process, was addressed with an assigned mentor and assessed for inclusion in the methodological section of the research study (Patton, 2002).

Organization of the Remainder of the Study

Chapter 1's overview noted the background of the problem and statement of the problem of parental treatment seeking experiences. The purpose and significance of the study were included to provide a basis for the study's development. The chapter outlined the research design of this study, presented the assumptions and limitations, and defined the terms. The end of the chapter concluded with research biases for consideration.

This study continued with a literature review as it relates to the topic of study. In Chapter 2 the literature review will begin by presenting the key features and etiology of ADHD then move into the exploration of Barkley's theory of self-regulation and executive function as it relates to ADHD. Further theoretical frameworks will include parent motivation and social stigma. This chapter will discuss the connection between ADHD and learning disabilities and parental experiences with the school system. The conclusion of the chapter will examine parental experience in seeking various treatment interventions.

The research methods used and the procedures implemented will be outlined in Chapter 3 of this study. There will be a discussion of the purpose of the study and the target population selection for participation. Included in this chapter will be the research questions and explanation of the data analysis. This section will close with ethical considerations.

Chapter 4 will detail the data collection and data analysis procedures. The incorporation of the verbatim responses of the parent participants will be presented to describe the experiences of seeking treatment for their children diagnosed with ADHD.

In Chapter 5 the research will be reviewed and the research study results will be presented. The research findings will be used to generate conclusions and guide suggestions for future research on the topic of parental experiences of seeking ADHD treatment.

CHAPTER 2. LITERATURE REVIEW

Introduction to the Literature Review

This research study examines parental experiences as they seek treatment for their children diagnosed with ADHD. The literature was examined using a number of keywords and databases in search of relevant scholarly journal articles. A literature search was conducted using the following: Academic Search Premier, CINAHL with Full Text, Education Research Complete, ERIC, Ovid Nursing Full Text PLUS, ProQuest Education Journals, ProQuest Medical Library, ProQuest Psychology Journals, PsycARTICLES, PsycINFO, PubMed Central, SAGE Journals Online, ScienceDirect, SocINDEX with Full Text, and Summon. The topics were separated by keywords such as: Parents, Perceptions, Perceive, Belief, Attitude, Children, and attention deficit hyperactivity disorder.

In this chapter, readers have found a comprehensive literature review that correlates with the topic of study. In the beginning of the review, the researcher broadly introduced the topic of ADHD and then move into Dr. Russell Barkley's theory of self-regulation and executive function as it is applicable to ADHD. Diagnosing ADHD and the prevalence of comorbidity between ADHD and other diagnoses will be explored. The connection between ADHD and learning disabilities was detailed and the literature review concluded with parental experiences with ADHD and seeking treatment.

Theoretical Orientation for the Study

One theory used to focus the inquiry, analyze data, and to critique the results, was Dr. Barkley's executive function and self-regulation theory of ADHD. A wider scope of the issue of the executive function was examined and included in presentation. Barkley introduced his theoretical perspective of self-regulation and executive function, and ADHD following the work of Virginia Douglas. This theory took interest in identifying the neurobiological implications of ADHD symptomology rather than focusing on the social and behavioral contributing factors. There were clinical researchers as early as the 1970's, such as Virginia Douglas who began to make the connection between ADHD and self-regulation (Douglas, 1972).

There were two overlying components to Barkley's theory on ADHD and they included self-regulation and executive function. Self-regulation is described as the key problem which directly impacts executive function. Barkley uses the terms self-regulation and executive function interchangeably and sums up ADHD as a problem of self-regulation (Hathaway & Barkley, 2003). There are four areas of executive function which are impacted by deficits in behavioral inhibitions: non-verbal working memory, internalization of speech, emotional self-regulation, and reconstitution. The basis for such behavioral deficits is attributed largely to genetic and neuro-developmental influences as opposed to solely social factors (Hathaway & Barkley, 2003). This was a key component with Barkley's theory over previous theorists who attributed ADHD in large part to social and behavioral problems.

Theoretical Orientation of Social Stigma

Another theoretical orientation to this study was social stigma and how it affected treatment seeking behaviors and experiences. Many times there is a stigma associated with mental health diagnosis and treatment. Where there was labeling, discriminating, and loss of status, stereotyping and exclusion ... there was the social phenomenon of stigma (dosReis, Barksdale, Sherman, Maloney, & Charach, 2010). Some research related to treatment seeking among individuals with ADHD has shown social stigma was a strong contributing factor for preventing pursuit of treatment (dosReis et al., 2010). Stigmatizing beliefs, overmedicating children for behavioral disorders, and long-term developmental effects on children who accept medication are all negative perspectives to treatment which could serve as barriers for parents deciding to seek intervention services (dos Reis et al., 2010).

ADHD places affected individuals at heightened risk of experiencing prejudice, discrimination, and various forms of stigma (Mueller et al., 2012). In the article by Mueller et al. (2012) researchers examined existing literature as it related to stigma associated with ADHD. There were 33 articles selected to be included in the review. Their work was categorized into four areas of ADHD stigma: in children, in adults, in close relatives, and in the attitudes of those in authority towards the diagnosed individual (Mueller et al., 2012). The researchers found there was several contributing factors to the development of stigma which created risk factors for those diagnosed with ADHD. Some of the variables contributing to stigma were the reliability/validity of the disorder and how the diagnostic assessment determined the presence of ADHD (Mueller et al., 2012). Another variable consisted of skepticism the public holds regarding ADHD treatment and the use of medication and medication disclosure issues. The impact of stigma and ADHD has been underestimated and impacts the risk factors of those diagnosed with the disorder (Mueller et al., 2012). The stigma associated risk factors include treatment adherence and efficacy outcomes, symptomologies presentation, overall life satisfaction, and one's mental stability (Mueller et al.,

2012). Stigma has been defined by Corrigan and Shapiro (2010) as a concept largely influenced by cultural beliefs, which may shift yet are generally persistent environmental stressors.

Mueller et al. (2012) discussed three features of stigma: public, self, and courtesy. Public stigma accepts the negative attributes or stereotypes about ADHD by the dominant group and further ostracizes those diagnosed individuals (Corrigan & Shapiro, 2010). Self-stigma is when an individual begins to internalize the negative stigma held by others and assumes such as their new identity and therefore impacts them socially (Fabrega, 1990). Courtesy stigma is often experienced by parents of children with ADHD; as friends and family, who are closest to the diagnosed person, begins to experience negative judgment (dosReis et al., 2010).

One way that ADHD stigma is formed is through the media and press when they report an unbalanced view of the negative attributes of ADHD and treatment efforts (Schmitz, Filippone, & Edelman, 2003). The message produced by the media directly impacted concerns presented by parents regarding treatment (dosReis, et al., 2010). In one study, 21% of

parents held negative beliefs; stigma, about ADHD
treatment due to media influences (dosReis, et al.,
2010). Those stigmatizing beliefs were directed
towards the adverse effects of treatment, the risk
factors for substance abuse, and impact on the quality
of life for children and adolescents with ADHD
(dosReis et al., 2010).

Theoretical Orientation of Parent Motivation

There can be a variety of barriers or factors
that influence parental motivation to participate in their
child's ADHD treatment. Some of the contributing
factors to motivation found in the literature include
behavior parent training, culture, school systems, and
stigma (Arcia & Fernandez, 1998; Fabiano, 2007;
Hervey-Jumper, Douyon, Franco, Peters, & Jackson,
2006).

One commonly recommended treatment for
ADHD is behavioral parent training (BPT) (Fabiano,
2007). The treatment method has been
recommended for more than 40 years (Fabiano,
2007). BPT's serve the purpose of providing parents
with psycho-education about responding to triggers,

responding appropriately with consequences, and targeting adverse behaviors (Fabiano, 2007). One factor that has been demonstrated in the literature is lack of involvement with BPT's; demonstrated by not adhering to training models, poor attendance, never attending, discontinuing early, arriving late, and incomplete homework assignments (Barkley et al., 2000; Cunningham, Davis, Bremner, Dunn, & Rzasa, 1993; Fabiano, 2007).

Fabiano (2007) conducted a literature review of 32 studies examining fathers' participation in BPT treatment. One of the suggestions is to target behavioral training towards effective disciplinary responses and improving parenting skills (Fabiano, 2007). In a study with fathers and child actors who portrayed behaviors typical of ADHD, it was noted fathers often expressed feelings of being stressed, depressed mood, anxiety, and increased hostility (Pelham et al., 1997, 1998). The fathers further saw their ability to manage and respond to the child actors' behaviors as unsuccessful and lacking the effectiveness needed to modify the behavior. Fabiano (2007) described several areas which may assist in understanding the lack of parent motivation in ADHD treatment, specific to fathers. ADHD has a strong biological component, with parents being more likely to have ADHD when they have a child diagnosed with the disorder (Biederman, Faraone, & Monuteaux, 2002). Parental ADHD has been found to impact the effective parenting practices and treatment outcomes relevant to BPT (Sonuga-Barke, Daley, & Thompson, 2002). Another factor found to influence fathers' motivation is the structuring of the BPT classes. Fabiano (2007) discussed the classroom style of teaching, the availability of classes, and the marginalization of the father's input from the intake through treatment recommendation process, as examples of negatively impacting fathers' motivation.

Kazantzis, Deane, and Ronan (2000) found in their research study that parents who were consistent in practicing homework assignments showed improvement in their overall parenting practices than parents who were inconsistent with homework implementation. It is important for fathers to find a meaningful connection to the material being presented in BPT and the value of it as a treatment modality if there are to be any gains in parenting practices (Fabiano, 2007). Some father's lack motivation for BPT because it may be framed in a way that highlights their parenting skills deficiencies or they simply do not see themselves in need of parenting education (Fabiano, 2007).

Some research has found parent motivation to be largely influenced by a parent's culture which aides in developing ADHD schema (Arcia & Fernandez, 1998). ADHD research consistently demonstrates lower utilization rates of ADHD treatment among African Americans compared to their Caucasian counterparts (Eiraldi, Mazzuca, Clarke, & Power, 2006). Chen, Seipp, and Johnston (2008) found ethnicity/culture has been found to influence some parents' motivation to engage in treatment because of their attribution beliefs. Bussing, Gary, Mills, and Garvan (2007) found that practitioners should improve cultural competence approaches, when discussing explanatory models and treatment recommendations for ADHD, with African American families.

Parent treatment motivation was found to be influenced by the parents' perception of the school's response to ADHD symptoms. Hervey-Jumper et al. (2006) found a direct correlation between a parents' perception of the school as unhelpful and their hesitancy to accept the diagnosis and utilize a medication treatment regimen. Dreyer, O'Laughlin, Moore, and Milam (2010) found in their research the most cited reason for lack of parent motivation was how the parent perceived the child's teacher was in their willingness to implement the interventions.

Stigma has been a common thread among some parents, guiding their help seeking behaviors (Mueller et al., 2012). In one study women reported feeling blamed by others for their child's ADHD behaviors and engaged in self-blame (Peters & Jackson, 2009). The women further reported being stigmatized on various levels and perceived themselves as being socially rejected. In social and self-stigma, parents are less likely to be motivated to engage in intervention services.

There are a number of factors influencing parent motivation for ADHD from gender, race and cultural values, to parental expectations, how BPT's are structured, ADHD knowledge, and social stigma (Eiraldi et al., 2006). Practitioners who seek to remove such barriers and challenges to treatment have the opportunity to assist in improving parent motivation for treatment for ADHD.

Review of Research Literature Specific
to the Topic or Research Question

Diagnosing ADHD

ADHD is one of the most commonly treated childhood disorders in the United States with 3% - 7% of all school age children are diagnosed with the disorder (Stroh, Frankenberger, Cornell-Swanson, Wood, & Pahl, 2008). The disorder is commonly noted to appear during childhood and more specifically as the child enters school and/or the first several years of their academic career (Goldman, Genel, Bezman, & Slanetz, 1998). While the previous school of thought was, the disorder dissipated as the child aged, it is well documented many children will continue with symptoms throughout adolescence and beyond (Goldman et al., 1998). ADHD has specific criteria one must meet to receive the clinical diagnosis. Some of the characteristics of ADHD are hyperactivity, inattention, and impulsivity which are demonstrated in various settings (Moen, Hall-Lord, & Hedelin, 2011). The research clearly demonstrates there is a higher rate of prevalence among boys than with girls with one reason being that boys often demonstrate externalizing symptoms while girls show internalizing symptoms (Moen et al., 2011). When determining if a child meets the criteria for ADHD, it is a licensed medical or mental health professional who has the authority to make such diagnosis. The licensed professional will determine if the behaviors are age appropriate, assess the frequency of the symptoms, along with the severity of such (Bussing, Zima, Gary, & Wilson-Garvan, 2003). ADHD has a high comorbidity rate with other disorders along with many other impairments in daily living, such as risk of accidents, social acceptance, and impaired parental relationships (Chen, Seipp, & Johnston, 2008). ADHD further influences familial stability, emotional well-being, and requires an increase call of attention on the part of the parents (Peters & Jackson, 2009). There are a variety of treatment recommendations for ADHD to include medication, changes in diet and supplements, behavioral modifications, psychotherapy, and pharmacotherapy (Peters & Jackson, 2009). Additional interventions include parenting workshops focused on parenting skills, behavioral supports to be used within the school system, and programs during the summer to concentrate on building social relationships (Dreyer, O'Laughlin, Moore, & Milam, 2010). Due to the passage of legislation and advocacy groups, there has been an increase in students receiving supportive services in schools through 504 Accommodations (Eiraldi et al., 2006). The accommodations granted through a 504 allow for classroom and testing modifications and in-school counseling services to be provided to students who qualify for such.

ADHD Comorbidity

Although there has been great debate whether parents should medicate their children with ADHD or not, there is evidence that shows the considerable effects of not treating ADHD. As discussed there are several disorders that are often presented alongside ADHD symptoms. Conduct disorder, psychiatric conditions, academic impairment, and family system challenges, all have a high comorbidity rate with ADHD (Goldman et al., 1998). Untreated ADHD symptoms also leaves individuals at high risk for substance abuse, depression, anxiety, and learning disabilities (Bailey & Owen, 2005). Burns and Walsh (2002) describe the connection between ADHD and conduct problems to be so closely linked as a result of the hyperactivity and impulsivity in ADHD, which often precipitates the onset of conduct problems. Some of the symptoms found in some children who are not treated for their ADHD are substance abuse, academic difficulties and failure, and encounters with the juvenile justice system (Mills, 2011). Oppositional Defiant Disorder (ODD) and/or Conduct Disorder (CD) is the second most common reason that parents seek treatment for their children (Maniadaki, Sonuga-Barke, Kakouros, & Karaba, 2006). Some of the key symptoms with ODD are a negativistic disposition, oppositional, and hostile behavior (American Psychiatric Association, 2013).

Maniadaki et al. (2006) examined the causal attributions that parents held regarding ADHD and conduct problems. They wanted to see if there were differing causal attributions and how that impacted the parents' responses to the child's behavior. They also looked at maternal perceptions of the two disorders and then compared the reactions of the mothers to the behaviors. There were 317 participants in the study. All were mothers of children between the ages of 4-6 years old who attended either pre-school or kindergarten. The participants answered a questionnaire where they read a vignette describing behavior of a boy or girl, then answered a set of questions using a Likert scale examining parental perceptions. The authors used a between subject design and random assignment of mothers between the four groups. Factor analysis was used in the data analysis process then concluded with a multifactorial analyses of variance (ANOVAs). The results showed there was a stark difference in parental response between ADHD and conduct problems. Parents were less likely to respond in a punitive way to ADHD behaviors than to conduct problems. One of the conclusions found in the study is that parents had more tolerance for hyperactivity and other ADHD symptoms than for oppositional and defiant behaviors. Parents often looked at the behaviors as two separate entities which could lead to parents who discipline children for behaviors which they do not have the ability to control. In converse parents who are not able to distinguish between what a child cannot do and what they will not do may often overlook behaviors, which should be corrected. The causal attribution for ADHD was more often seen as a neurobiological factor while conduct problems were often attributed to willful misconduct on the part of the child.

ADHD and Learning Disabilities

ADHD continues to have a frequent rate of comorbidity with learning disabilities, affecting ones academic performance and impeding upon one's educational success (Dorneles et al., 2014). The research has shown that ADHD tends to affect a child and adolescent in similar ways as a learning disability, such as impairments in listening comprehension and working memory (McInnes, Humphries, Hogg-Johnson, & Tannock, 2003). One of the interventions noted in working with children with ADHD are school-based treatments (Barkley, 2007). Those school-based interventions can often address the behavioral and emotional components of a student as well as the organizational and academic (Barkley, 2007).

The Individuals with Disabilities Education Improvement Act (IDEA) of 2004 is a federal law allowing for the provision of special education services to children and adolescents who meet the criteria for having a disability (Maki, Floyd, & Roberson, 2015). Learning disabilities fall within the scope of special education services in school systems. There are various ways across the states which practitioners are evaluating children and adolescents for special education services. Some states continue to use the ability-achievement discrepancy model, while others are using Response to Intervention (RtI), or Processing Strengths and Weaknesses (PSW) models (Maki et al., 2015). One of the draw backs from having different models is the lack of consistency from state-to-state. Those inconsistencies account for the discrepancy for which children are identified for services and what meets the eligibility criteria from state-to-state (Maki et al., 2015).

The term Learning Disabilities (LD) was coined in the 1960's however clinicians and researchers were studying such conditions well before that time (Mash & Barkley, 2007). Working memory deficits have been found in persons with ADHD and those with learning disabilities. The working memory allows the temporary storage and manipulation of information which is vital for complex cognitive tasks such as comprehension, learning, and reasoning (Martinussen & Major, 2011). With this area of the brain being affected by those with ADHD it becomes clearer how ADHD and LD become connected. There are ways that can assist students with ADHD. Adapting instruction, providing external supports to reduce working memory load and teaching goal-oriented behaviors are a few interventions (Martinussen & Major, 2011). The complimentary patterns between ADHD and LD can also be viewed in the reverse. Similar to the incidents of ADHD, children who have learning disabilities are also children with learning disabilities who have difficulties with attention and behavior (Dongil et al., 2011). In fact, the incidence of learning disabilities in children with attention deficit hyperactivity disorder is considerably high and has been reported to be between 9 to 25% (Kaufman & Nuerk, 2008).

The article by Kaufmann and Nuerk (2008) discusses the prevalence of academic difficulties among children with ADHD. The researchers examine the connection of basic number processing deficits in children and adolescents with ADHD. Multivariate analyses of variance were conducted with group membership (ADHD-C vs. control) as a between group factor. The assessment of intellectual functioning, and attentional resources, were provided on the first day together with the clinical interview of the child and the parents. The experimental tasks were given on a second day. Thirty-two right-handed children participated in this study. The experimental group (16 children with a diagnosis of ADHD-C) and the control group (16 children without ADHD) were similar in age and gender. The findings emphasize that inhibitory deficiencies seem to be a key factor of ADHD children as well as indicate the impact of different task requirements on the performance of cognition. Further evidence shows a link between low arithmetic achievement and deficient attention. Children with ADHD-C did show difficulties in tasks related to non-verbal number magnitude representation.

Doyle, Biederman, Seidman, Weber, and Faraone, (2000) discuss the differences between boys with and without ADHD on neuropsychological tests. The results on neuropsychological tests have been shown to be predictive of ADHD. An empirical approach was used examining the feasibility of neuropsychological tests in differentiating children with ADHD from non-ADHD controls. The authors used several tests of attention and executive functioning to examine boys with and without ADHD. This research analyzes the results from a 4-year follow-up longitudinal study of ADHD. The subjects were 6–17-year-old males with vs. without ADHD. Subjects were referred by parents, pediatricians, and schools for psychiatric evaluations. Normal controls were selected from each setting from pediatric clinics. Results demonstrated that children with ADHD tend to demonstrate deficiencies on neuropsychological tests of attention and executive functions. Furthermore, impairments on multiple neuropsychological tests are indicative of ADHD, while normal scores do not rule out the diagnosis (Doyle et al., 2000).

In the article by Shallice et al. (2002) the researchers examined the neuropsychological profile for executive functions in children diagnosed with ADHD to assess the association with inhibition and attentional problems. This was an empirical study. There were a number of tasks: sustained attention reaction time task, related vigilance task, sentence completion task, spatial rule attainment task, letter fluency task, number Stroop task, and an "n-back" working memory task (Shallice et al., 2002). The sample involved 31 children with ADHD and 33 normal controls aged 7 to 12 years. Children were recruited from primary schools. Study results confirmed abnormalities in the domain of inhibitory processes: attentional functions, and executive functions, of the ADHD group (Shallice et al., 2002). The ADHD group was severely impacted in strategy generation and use.

Litner and Mann-Feder, (2009) reviews the implications of recent research for interventions with youth with ADHD and Learning Disabilities (LD).This is a qualitative study, where volunteers were interviewed to learn more about the factors that played a key role in positively affecting the educational attainment, academic success, and social integration of these students. Subjects were students in their classes who had managed to come to the university. The research setting was in the university. Findings suggest the personalities of the students and internal factors had a greater impact on resilience than external supports. Additionally, students from both groups were described by internal strengths and such traits were paramount in preserving resilience.

ADHD and LD do have some specific common features while at the same time many children and adolescents who exhibit ADHD behaviors, can also be found to have a learning disability once evaluated. While such population is classified with a learning disability, they often have attentional and behavioral issues (Mash, 2007). Many of the selected articles remarked about the incidents of ADHD combined with a learning disability. Most articles mentioned executive function and explained how that is significant in understanding ADHD. Some articles focused on specific areas of executive function, such as working memory that is needed for complex learning, mathematics, and learning new information. This provides insight explaining why children with ADHD have difficulties in the areas of reading comprehension and mathematics.

Parental Experience with Treatment Choices for ADHD

There are a number of treatment options for ADHD which include traditional and a growing use of alternative treatments. Some of the traditional forms of treatment include medication, behavioral management, and school-based treatment such as accommodations to support student success (Pellow, Solomon, & Barnard, 2011). Although medication is the number one treatment recommendation for ADHD, parents are being led to seek complementary and alternative medical therapies (CAM) due to concerns about side-effects, long-term medication use, and preferring to avoid medication treatment (Pellow et al., 2011). Some of the alternative treatments being sought by parents are diet, exercise therapy, supplemental interventions, herbal and homeopathic treatment (Pellow et al., 2011). Pellow et al. (2011) report that CAM gives parents options beyond traditional treatments for ADHD and some have the potential to provide a beneficial outcome in treating the child's symptoms.

Johnston, Seipp, Hommersen, and Fine (2005) conducted research exploring the connection between the beliefs and attitudes of parents and their child's ADHD treatment experience. Parents' choice in treatment is often guided by their beliefs about treatment and causal factors of ADHD (Johnston et al., 2005). There were 73 Canadian parents of boys ages 5-13 years old who all had a medical diagnosis of ADHD. The parents completed questionnaires then researchers later analyzed the data using within-participant analyses of variance, divided the samples, used analyses of variance for comparative purposes, and used a 0.05 level of significance (Johnston et al., 2005). This study found there were varied treatment modalities parents were engaging in and such practices appeared to be the norm for parents with a child with ADHD (Johnston et al., 2005). Parents in this study reported using several types of ADHD treatments: diet/vitamins, behavior management, school, child/family psychotherapy, and medication. The parents in this sample predominantly used medication and behavior management to treat ADHD and report the experience on the effectiveness scale as being above average. The school-based help was reported by half of the sample and experienced as helpful. There were one-half of the participants who utilized alternative methods to treating their child's ADHD, with diet and vitamins being the most common. Parents rated their experience with this method as below average as it relates to effectiveness (Johnston et al., 2005). The challenges expressed for medication was the unwanted side effects and the sometimes-exhaustive efforts of behavior management. There were about one fourth of parents who engaged in child/family therapy and rated their experience with such as below average for effectiveness.

The partnership between family and school is pivotal when attempting to address the challenges of ADHD (Power et al., 2012). In the study by Power et al. (2012), the authors focused on implementing interventions aimed at improving the family and educational functioning of students (Power et al., 2012). The study targeted children in grades 2-6 diagnosed with ADHD and used a 12-week psychosocial approach to improving Family-School Success (FSS). This was a quantitative study that analyzed the data using a linear mixed effects regression model at two stages; post-intervention and follow-up (Power et al., 2012). The main aspects of FSS were behavioral consultations, behavioral homework interventions, and use of daily report cards (Power et al., 2012). The study concluded that FSS was successful in improving the school-home relationship, improved performance on homework, and in measures of parental behavior (Power et al., 2012). Parents experienced FSS favorably as an acceptable method for improving the areas of concern (Power et al., 2012). The school system is a key area where behavioral interventions are employed to address academic issues (Power et al., 2012). It is important to understand which school-based interventions are helpful in minimizing adverse behaviors. Throughout the literature, behavioral training for parents is noted as a crucial aspect in working with children with ADHD, to see improvement at school and home (Fabiano et al., 2009). Activities that include interactions between both systems: ensuring homework is completed, assisting as needed, and collaborative efforts to address concerns as they surface; are all attributable to student success (Fantuzzo, Tighe, & Childs, 2000).

Various interventions have been found in the literature that attempt to improve school and parental experience in working with students with ADHD. Parental behavioral training, organizational and social skills training, and daily report cards were introduced over a two-year period by Abikoff et al. (2004). The parenting behavioral training focused on teaching parents how to respond effectively to ADHD behaviors, while school staff provided students with the skills to assist in organizing themselves at both home and school, and teaching how to foster positive social relationships. The daily report cards were used to communicate with the parents how the students performed in school on a particular day. Another study used parent training as the basis of the intervention coupled with teacher consultation, and child skills training, and found it was effective in addressing organizational skills in those research participants (Pfiffner et al., 2007). Owens, Murphy, Richerson, Grio, and Himawan (2008) developed an intervention using parent training, daily report cards, and behavioral consultation to teachers and demonstrated reduced symptomology and impaired conditions while improving parental and teacher relationships with the students. Conjoint Behavioral Consultation (CBC) focuses on the collaborative efforts between parents and schools and has been an effective measure used to work with behavioral challenges and educational impairment (Power et al., 2012).

In the article by Johnston, Mah, and Regambal (2010) they performed a study to examine how parental beliefs about their ability to manage their child's behavior and their treatment beliefs correlated with parental treatment experience outcomes. There were 101 mothers who participated with children from 5-10 years of age. Mothers conveyed their beliefs about their effectiveness in managing their child's behavior and behavioral attributions (Johnston et al., 2010). The mothers completed questionnaires, rating scales, evaluation inventories, and structured interviews (Johnston et al., 2010). Results were examined descriptively, assessed for multivariate outliers, an exploratory factor analysis was performed, a principal component analysis with varimax rotation included, and then finally researchers tested the structural modeling (Johnston et al., 2010).

The research did conclude that beliefs of parenting efficacy did contribute to the overall parent treatment experience specifically as it relates to Behavioral Parenting Training (BPT). If a parent had a positive perception about their ability to parent their child with ADHD they were likely to have a positive experience with BPT (Johnston et al., 2010). In this study, as mothers' perceived their abilities as competent it was more likely they believed behavioral interventions were an effective resource and reported their experience as more successful as they used them more often (Johnston et al., 2010). Some of the suggestions made were to improve parental perceptions of efficacy prior to beginning BPT.

In the research by Efron, Sciberras, and Hassell (2008) they examined parental perceptions of teacher understanding, information available, and school supports provided as they relate to children with ADHD. This was a quantitative study conducted in Australia using parent participants who had a child between 6-19 years old. The results of the study found that parents experience the teacher's understanding of ADHD as inadequate, and the information and school supports as insufficient. The researchers point to a limitation of the study as not examining the level of understanding of the teachers, but rather the parents' perception of such. However, the researchers refer to other studies which have examined teacher knowledge of ADHD and say such research is supportive of their findings (Efron et al., 2008). Parents did not feel the information available to help their children with their ADHD symptoms was sufficient.

In the article by Brinkman and Epstein (2011) they reviewed the literature on parental experience with physicians in treating ADHD. The vital components in this parent-physician relationship includes providing information to the family, setting treatment goals, formulating a treatment plan, cardiovascular screening, titrating[1] medication, and continuous treatment plan monitoring and revising (Brinkman & Epstein, 2011). The article focused on the physician-parent interactions for the main components of care, assessed the current practices, and examined challenges to providing these practices. One study of 11,674 parents, showed that

---

[1] *Titrating helps the body adapt to a medication; it also helps physician and patient find the optimal dose to improve daily functioning; the doctor will increase the dose slowly to the highest tolerable or most beneficial dose.*

79% believed that needed information was 'usually' or 'always' provided to them, 78% said physicians spend enough time with them, 87% 'listen carefully', and 88% were culturally sensitive (Brinkman & Epstein, 2011). One of the limitations of the study was there were no audio or visual tapes to review. Brinkman and Epstein (2011) described the use of audio and/or visual tapes as essential for any significant gains in this respect. The tapes would show to what extent options are provided, pros and cons are discussed, goals are set but not documented, and parent treatment preferences and values are prompted (Brinkman & Epstein, 2011). Recommendations for future study suggest incorporating audio/visual tapes to be reviewed, so the content can be screened to ensure the necessary components have been included as it relates to the collaborative effort of engaging parents in the treatment planning process (Brinkman & Epstein, 2011).

There is a wealth of research provided in journals on the topic of parental experience in using medication in treating their child's ADHD. Medication treatment continues to be the number one recommendation for treating symptoms of ADHD, and psycho-stimulant medications in particular have shown to be highly effective. There are approximately 3.5 million United States children and adolescents who are prescribed and use stimulant medications (Mills, 2011). Charach, Yeung, Volpe, Goodale, and dosReis (2014) conducted research that examined both the beliefs and attitudes of the use of medication and how parental influences determine treatment factors. In their study, the participants were young adolescents (12) and their parent counterparts (12). They were each interviewed separated, resulting in 24 interviews. The data was collected through qualitative interviews allowing participants in-depth responses to open ended questions. The interviews were recorded and later transcribed. The researchers looked for patterns, themes, and meaning in those interviews. Researchers would take turns reviewing each document and wherever there was a discrepancy, the researchers would discuss such until a consensus was met amongst them. Some of the attitudes about the medication were benefits, effects on sense of self, adverse effects, and desire to discontinue (Charach et al., 2014). This research study showed the differences between parental and young adolescents' perspectives on the use of medication. It also highlights that ones' beliefs and attitudes towards medication will greatly impact their adherence to a medication regimen. It is important to include young people in the treatment planning process as they begin to take an active role in their medication and treatment adherence. In cases where the young adolescent is not consulted with or included in the treatment plan, the follow through with such recommendation may show poorly. However, when young adolescents are included there is great opportunity to mitigate any questions, misconceptions, and/or issues. The parental experience in seeking treatment can be impacted by how such treatment is viewed to begin with.

Pham, Carlson, and Kosciulek (2010) found there were not significant ethnic differences of how parents viewed the origin of ADHD. They conducted a quantitative study with119 parents who completed a questionnaire with the research goal of examining if there were ethnic differences among parental beliefs regarding the origin of ADHD and furthermore if such beliefs determine the treatment parents are likely to seek. The parents initially completed a survey and later a 36-item questionnaire that incorporated a 5-point Likert-type scale. The researchers included two qualitative, open-response questions to gather the beliefs of the contributing factors of ADHD and preferences for treatment (Pham et al., 2010). The study included 58 parents who had children with a diagnosis of ADHD and sixty-one parents without a child with ADHD. The parents were ethnically diverse and all had children between the ages of 5-12 years-old. The authors used the following methods of data analysis to include analysis of covariance, content analysis, and multinomial logistical regression. The authors found African Americans were less likely than Caucasian counterparts to see the significant role their child's school can play in ADHD identification and they shared less concern about how ADHD symptoms connect to school-based problems. Pham et al. (2010) stressed the need for schools to be more diligent in their culturally competent parent education on the topic of ADHD. Schools have the opportunity to provide psycho-education to parents informing them of evidence based treatment, explaining the causes of ADHD, and providing community resources to address the symptoms and supportive services a family may need. Oftentimes it is the school system advising the parent for the first time that there is a clinical concern with their child. A parents' quest for treatment may begin at the school in inquiries for school-based services and support. How the school responds to that parent can have a significant positive or adverse effect on their first steps towards treatment. Even parents with the best intentions to assist their child may be met with obstacles. There are many barriers and challenges that can come up for a family who is attempting to obtain treatment services for their child's ADHD. Bailey and Owen (2005) describe some of those barriers to consist of providers who are culturally competent in addressing the needs and nuances specific to ethnic groups, financial limitations, and a lack of ADHD information provided to families. These barriers have been included in the study as recommendations for future research.

Stroh et al. (2008) provided research on the topic of parental knowledge, attitudes, and treatment for ADHD. There were 146 participants which contained parents who had children in elementary school. The study involved the use of a survey followed by a 58-item questionnaire with a 5-point Likert scale. There were two questions contained that sought to explore how that parent came to the decision to seek the treatment they have for their child's ADHD. Another two questions focused on those professionals most influential in directing the treatment decision. One of the key findings in this study was doctors were the most influential factor on parent's treatment decision (48.3%) followed by teachers (24.1%) (Stroh et al., 2008). The research also suggested the parents were not well-informed about the ADHD treatment with medication and treatment specific to behavioral programs. Parents generally lacked knowledge of the benefits of each and held beliefs about them which were inaccurate. Parents were also unaware of the adverse outcomes on certain areas such as motor tics, future drug addiction, and developmental growth. The research also demonstrated a stark difference between those parents with a child diagnosed with ADHD and those without when beliefs of medication views were explored. Those parents with a child diagnosed with ADHD were more favorable towards this intervention than those parents without a child diagnosed with

ADHD. The study suggests parents of a child with ADHD were more likely informed about medication benefits from their doctor's office literature. Much of that literature is published by pharmaceutical companies and therefore medication would be presented more favorably which in turn begins to shape the views of parents engaging in such treatment. Finally, the research study showed that parents often relied on biased information such as pamphlets from doctors' offices, for their treatment decisions. When examining the parental experience of seeking treatment one may assume that if the only option given for treatment is medication and the parent is strictly opposed to medication, that may hinder their quest to purse any treatment. Teachers and school systems can benefit families considerably by becoming informed about the symptoms of ADHD, evidenced based treatment recommendations for such, and community resources for the families they engage with. Bussing et al. (2007) reported that schools should become better agents at informing parents of effective intervention strategies, within the school system, that could best serve students with ADHD.

Mills (2011) did a study that focused on the decision-making process of parents in deciding if they would utilize medication or not as part of their child's treatment regimen. There were 19 parents who participated. All participants had a child medically diagnosed with ADHD. The parents were selected from a purposeful sample to participate in this qualitative study. The data was collected through audiotaped, semi-structured interviews which were later transcribed. A question-by-question and later line-by-line analysis were conducted. The researcher then probed the data further by performing a phrase and single word analysis (Mills, 2011). The researcher's observations were written after each interview session. The results of the study found there to be no significant difference among the groups: medicated and not medicated, in their decision-making processes. The parental experiences with the medical professionals varied among the group of participants. Some felt the doctors were thorough in gathering information from parent interviews, medical tests, checklists, interviews, and assessments while others reported an ADHD diagnosis was given after a brief meeting.

Review of Methodological Literature Specific
to the Topic or Research Question

In the process of conducting the literature review, there were several articles found that support the methodological model detailed in this research study. Some of the key supporting literature described the benefits of using a qualitative study to probe this type of research question (Charach & Gajaria, 2008). There were a number of research studies on parental experience with ADHD and or experience with medication that incorporated some or all of these research methods: semi-structured interviews, transcribing sessions verbatim, the use of member checking, and incorporating a line-by-line data analysis (dosReis et al., 2009; dosReis, Barksdale, Sherman, Maloney, & Charach, 2010; Mills, 2011). In the research performed by Mills (2011), the research was conducted through the use of qualitative means as she explored the decision making patterns of parents in deciding to use medication for their children's ADHD diagnosis. Her research included semi-structured interviews for gathering information, audiotapes were transcribed and shared with participants to check for accuracy, and analyzed data using a line-by-line analysis. This methodology supports the research question by being able to gather responses of what factors were used in the parental decision-making experience.

Pham et al. (2009) gathered information about parental preferences to treatment and beliefs of ADHD causes using open-response questions. Charach et al. (2014) used a qualitative methodology as they conducted interviews of adolescents and their parents. The research examined the participants' beliefs about ADHD, the use of stimulant medications, and the parental decision making process. Semi-structured interviews were employed and the researchers continued to gather data until there were no further emergence of new themes regarding beliefs and attitudes about ADHD and the use of medication. In the research by Brinkman et al. (2009) the researchers used a qualitative methodology in exploring parental decision making about ADHD treatment. In their study, they utilized focus groups, transcribed verbatim the sessions, and then later coded the interview by common themes.

dosReis, Mychailyszyn, Myers, and Riley
(2007) used a qualitative approach to interviewing
participants by phone, then transcribing interviews
verbatim. A line-by-line analysis was conducted and
data was analyzed within and across participant
interviews. This process was continued until
saturation was met; evidenced by no new data. This
research examined how urban African American
parents decide which treatment modality to seek for
their children's ADHD.

Morton, Tong, Howard, Snelling, and Webster
(2013) found one of the possible benefits of
synthesizing qualitative work is the ability to gain
information on such research questions pertaining to
the experiences of the parents, what treatment
methods worked, for whom they worked, and the
circumstances allowing such treatment to work. Their
research examined the influential factors parents
faced in determining to use stimulant medication to
treat their child's ADHD symptoms. Charach and
Gajaria (2008) discuss the internal validity associated
with qualitative interviews conducted with parent
participants. The researchers argued that information
captured in a qualitative study could fill in the gaps

associated with the more common quantitative methodologies, and can therefore assist in providing new insight in treatment adherence (Charach & Gajaria, 2008). There are a number of studies that support the methodology and approaches that this researcher designed in this dissertation research plan. Some of the methodological support focuses on the use of a case study to capture in-depth meaning of parental experiences, semi-structured interviews that allow participants to share in a free flowing manner, recording interviews and transcribing verbatim, and a line-by-line data analysis that will examine patterns and meanings (dosReis et al., 2007; Morton et al., 2013; Pham et al., 2009).

Synthesis of the Research Findings

Dr. Barkley's executive function and self-regulation theory of ADHD is one of the constructs found within the literature regarding the theoretical model used for this dissertation, along with social stigma and parental motivation. In the model Dr. Barkley shifts from the generally accepted former beliefs that ADHD dealt primarily with behavior to an understanding of its neurologically-based disorder affecting the brain and ones inability to regulate behaviors as a result of such. Bailey and Owens (2005) describe ADHD as being a neuro-behavioral disorder, based in genetics, affecting the rate of release of dopamine and norepinephrine in the frontal lobe of the brain. This theory focuses on how the impaired executive function of those diagnosed with ADHD directly impacts their ability to self-regulate. With executive function being so widely used within psychological circles there are many variations of the definition of such and the literature lacks a concise meaning for this phenomenon.

The executive function component in the brain is key to one's ability to function efficiently in their day-to-day life and is used for problem-solving as one moves towards a goal (Barkley, 2006). In children and adolescents with ADHD it is this impairment that is often targeted within school settings for modifications such as providing prompts and organizational tools. The executive function helps one to be goal-directed while pursuing upcoming goals. The self-regulation component is used to modify ones' behavior to complete a goal or avoid consequences ones' behaviors may cause (Barkley, 2006). Barkley (2006) views this as a disabling feature within the individual with ADHD because they lack the neurological ability to gauge such. This view that ADHD is more of a neurologically based disorder has assisted in informing views that such behaviors were attributed to bad parenting or simply willful misconduct. It has been found views on ADHD develop from several sources with the main source being cultural. (Arcia & Fernandez, 1998). Culturally competent practitioners are needed in serving families with ADHD. Data will be collected, for this dissertation, with this in mind and parents are asked about how their cultural, religious, or other values played into their outlook on treatment for ADHD.

The research findings provide evidence that there is a direct link between social stigma and parent treatment seeking behaviors (dosReis et al., 2010). There are various types of social stigma; public, self, and courtesy (Mueller et al., 2012). Stigma is culturally constructed and viewed as a persistent environmental stressor (Corrigan & Shapiro, 2010). Self-stigma often is a result of either public or courtesy stigma that the individual then internalizes to become their way of viewing a condition; such as

ADHD. Any stigma creates risk factors for the targeted individual. Those risk factors include life satisfaction, mental stability, treatment continuity and efficacy outcomes, and the presentation of ADHD symptoms (Mueller et al., 2012). The role of stigma in treating ADHD is undervalued and influences other treatment experiences such as parental motivation (Mueller et al., 2012).

The literature on parental motivation showed there were a number of articles that examined parental motivation to participate in BPT's (Fabiano, 2007). The literature showed how culture influences both motivation and stigma. It also showed the interconnectivity between stigma and motivation. These constructs are at constant interplay and each has the ability to impact parental treatment seeking behaviors. The research consistently shows that African Americans do not engage in ADHD treatments at equal rates as their Caucasian counterparts (Eiraldi et al., 2006). School systems who partnered with the family assisted in parent motivation outcomes (Hervey-Jumper, Douyon, & Franco, 2006).

There is much to learn from this research as it provides depth of knowledge as to ethnic trends, demographics of parents who seek ADHD treatment, the effectiveness of such treatment, and more. For some parents who question the validity of ADHD they may also be less likely to use medication for a disorder they do not believe exists. The study conducted by Johnston et al. (2010) adds value by demonstrating how the beliefs of parental efficacy are predictive of parental treatment experience in parent training. One study found African American parents were less accepting of the ADHD diagnosis and medication treatment when they perceived the school system as being unhelpful (Hervey-Jumper et al., 2006). Another study highlighted implementing a family-school intervention withability to improve the overall quality of the relationship between both parties (Power et al., 2012). In studies presented examining parental experiences of the school resources, the main component was the implementation of parent training as a source for improving student success and encouraging pro-social behaviors. Despite the fact parent training is highly recommended for treating ADHD, utilization rates and consistency is limited (Johnston et al., 2010).

One of the recommendations provided from the research findings was to provide schools with more resources while providing additional training on the topic of ADHD to the teaching staff (Efron et al., 2008). Pham et al. (2010) highlights cultural competence as a needed component when schools interface with parents. One conclusion in the Mills (2011) study was that success in academics and school continued to be represented as the main beneficial reason for selecting medication. Also, misunderstandings between educators and parents contributed to conflicts between the parties. Sometimes educators did not have enough of a knowledge base on ADHD symptoms and treatment and misappropriated symptoms for malicious behaviors. Other times educators can become frustrated with the child and thereby contributing to the divide between the school and parent systems (Mills, 2011).

The article by Brinkman and Epstein (2011) adds value to this discussion by presenting the recommendations to physicians, by the American Academy of Pediatrics, for working with families who have a child diagnosed with ADHD. The areas that have not been addressed sufficiently can guide practitioners in their future practice with parents of children with ADHD. Practitioners should pursue becoming increasingly aware of the attitudes held in the communities in which they serve to help possibly improve communication, aide in decreasing behavioral symptoms, while improving treatment outcomes of the families they serve (Olaniyan et al., 2007). This study shows how influential both doctors and teachers are in a parent's treatment seeking experience.

The literature on untreated ADHD also includes the comorbidity of other disorders: conduct disorder, oppositional defiant disorder, learning disabilities, and mood disorders, and alcohol and drug dependency (Bailey & Owens, 2005). Charach and Gajaria (2008) found that treatment was dependent upon the presenting symptomology and prolonged treatment adherence was linked to the severity of symptoms.

The literature shows a variety of methods being used to include quantitative, qualitative, and mixed-methodologies. There were surveys, questionnaires, focus groups, and experiments used to gather insight into the parental experience with

ADHD treatment. While there were a number of articles to discuss a parents' experience with a choice of treatment, the gap in the literature surrounds a parents' treatment seeking experience. One of the distinctive advantages of the qualitative studies is the depth in the descriptive information provided by participants when answering research questions using a semi-structured model. Each methodology maintains its advantages and disadvantages. The use of a qualitative methodology for this dissertation study will allow for the rich and meaningful content as is evidenced by this study.

Critique of the Previous Research

There are notable gaps in the literature reviewed on parental experiences with ADHD treatment. Although there are articles on parents experience with various types of treatment, the literature is lacking in examining parental experience of seeking treatment. There are many types of treatments for ADHD, from traditional to alternative forms of treatment. Given the fact that parents often initiate treatment for their children it is essential to understand parental experience in seeking treatment

(Johnston et al., 2005). The study by Johnston et al. (2005) relates to this researcher's study by examining parental experience with ADHD treatment and their study highlights the need for the examination into this phenomenon. It is still unknown what the specific challenges are for parents as they seek treatment that would prevent them from continuing their pursuit of interventions for ADHD. This research attempts to address this gap in the literature.

The use of medication is controversial, which is the most common recommendation for the treatment of ADHD; stimulant medications such as methylphenidate (Hervey-Jumper et al., 2006). Medication is one of the most predominant controversies because the field is lacking longitudinal studies on children accepting ADHD medication (Charach & Gajaria, 2008). Despite the controversy surrounding medication use between 36-68% of young people who begin a medication regimen will continue such consistently with children accepting psycho-stimulants as their main source of ADHD treatment (Charach & Gajaria, 2008). Schmitz and Velez (2003) contend that the use of such medication in young children is highly debatable given the long-term effects the medication may cause.

The parental perceptions of ADHD are paramount as parents are in essence the gatekeepers between their child and ADHD treatment (Sayal, Taylor, Beecham, & Byrne, 2002). The article by Bussing et al. (2007) relates to this researcher's study by understanding where and how parental beliefs and views for treatment are formulated which impacts their experience. If the parent has negative beliefs about the disorder or recommended treatment modalities, this will impact the child's engagement in such treatment. For parents who question the validity of ADHD, the literature has shown where the presence of ADHD symptoms are, it is less likely to be identified as such within their children (Hervey-Jumper et al., 2006). In some cases it has been found that this perception is reinforced due to limited information provided to parents to inform their beliefs on this childhood disorder (Hervey-Jumper et al., 2006). In cases where the public questions the validity of the ADHD diagnosis, it has come up that there is no current defining evaluative test used to conclude the presence or absence of ADHD. Instead the basis for the ADHD diagnosis is provided as the practitioner performs a thorough history by obtaining information from the parents, the individuals, and collaterals such as school personnel who work with the child (Hervey-Jumper et al., 2006). The article by Mills (2011) adds to this researcher's study by reinforcing the work that is needed within school systems to adequately address the needs of students with ADHD and communicate the concerns in a manner likely to be received by parents. The article by Efron et al. (2008) adds value to this research study by showing areas for improvement when attempting to foster a positive school-home relationship for children diagnosed with ADHD. One of the main elements in assessing for ADHD are rating scales (Demaray, Elting, & Schaefer, 2003). Demaray et al. (2003) found that the Attention Deficit Disorder Evaluation Scales (ADDES), ADHD Rating Scale IV (ADHD-IV), and Conner's Rating Scale-Revised (CRS-R), are the most efficient rating scales for evaluating ADHD because of their reliability, validity, and standardization samples.

Barnard-Brak and Yen (2009) suggest as researchers examine parents who have treated their children's ADHD symptoms with medication that there should also be examinations into the parental nonresponse to treatment and what factors are present in such cases. Research shows that parent training plays a vital role in treating ADHD yet the number of parents participating is not reflective of the number of children diagnosed with ADHD (Owens et al., 2008). Chen and Johnston (2007) recommend practitioners to work with both parents when devising a treatment plan as there may be varying perceptions held among them regarding the nature and symptoms of ADHD.

The methodological trend in assessing parental experience with ADHD treatment in the literature appears to be quantitative studies using questionnaires, surveys, and focus groups. The benefits of this method are the ability to make generalizations. Some studies have used the ADHD Beliefs Scale while others used the Treatment History Questionnaire (Johnston et al., 2005). This type of method forces participants to deduct their responses to one that fits within the ratings of a Likert scale and does not allow for the individual meanings and nuances that come from a qualitative case study. The case study will better serve the need to gather information from parents on what their personal experiences entailed as they sought treatment for their child. Parents will not be bound to the data points on a rating scale and will be able to contribute as needed to open-ended semi- structured questions during an interview. The interviews will be conducted in person instead of over the phone as in some of the quantitative studies, allowing for this researcher to observe the unspoken body language of participants. The sample size in case studies is significantly smaller than those of quantitative works. For this reason, a case study finding is not easily generalizable. The strengths of a case study are to gather deep, meaningful information specific to that person's experience rather than to generalize with findings. The research instruments often used in quantitative works were evaluations that have been proven to be valid and credible in measuring the aspects they were used for in the studies. This study will use an interview guide created by this researcher for gathering in-depth understanding of the phenomenon of parental experience in seeking ADHD treatment. The three principles of data collection that assist in establishing validity and reliability of the case would be using multiple sources of evidence, creating a case study database, and maintaining a chain of evidence (Yin, 2009). Credibility will be safeguarded through researcher reflexivity, exploring data, developing themes, and assessing the relevance of all data provided to ensure it accurately represents the participants' experiences.

There were three theoretical frameworks used for this research. The first framework was Russell's Barkley's neuropsychological based theory involving self-regulation, executive function, and ADHD. This theory shifts from viewing ADHD as simply a behavior disorder and views it as a deficit in self-regulation affecting motivation, arousal, behavior control, moral reasoning, and reflection (Wallace, 2005). Another deficiency in this disorder is short term memory that allows for children to reflect to prior experiences to guide future decision making patterns (Wallace, 2005). Although the current study was not an examination of executive function and self-regulation, the critique is pertinent as it relates to this study's assumptions that ADHD is a brain based disorder that may therefore influence a parents' experience in seeking treatment. The second framework was social stigma and how it affects parental involvement with treatment and the treatment seeking experience. One of the research findings stated one way to decrease ADHD stigma was to increase the public's knowledge of ADHD through the media efforts (Schmitz et al., 2003). One of the overall findings as it relates to ADHD stigma is that treatment adherence and efficacy are directly related (Mueller et al., 2012). Recommendations were made to address the media in reporting accurate balanced stories on the subject of ADHD and treatment (Mueller et al., 2012). This research proposed can uncover clear reasons and parental understanding of the ADHD diagnosis experience. Some of the lessons learned from this inquiry could assist in acknowledging challenges to treatment; such as social stigma, and begin to address and improve such barriers. The third theoretical framework used in this study is parental motivation. BPT's are a valued part of the treatment recommendations for ADHD to be included in the treatment regimen. Fabiano (2007) found that to improve father motivation in ADHD BPT that barriers would need to be addressed: the structure of BPT, the content of the programs, the minimizing of father's input in the diagnostic process and treatment plan development, homework engagement, and father's finding the BPT to be a valued resource. Fabiano's (2007) research demonstrated several areas practitioners and future research could focus on in enhancing parental experience with BPT's while improving parental motivation. Future research should employ qualitative studies examining attitudes, beliefs, and perceptions to gain deeper insight of how such influences parent motivation to engage in ADHD treatment (Bussing et al., 2007). Parent motivation continues to be an area needing further research to examine the best methods for maintaining parental motivation for ADHD treatment.

Summary

ADHD symptoms are the most common reason parents seek treatment for their young children (Arcia & Fernandez, 1998). Studies examined the types of treatment methods and parental beliefs and perceptions of such, but no studies found specifically to examine the parental experience in seeking treatment for children with ADHD. Barkley's theory on ADHD and how it relates to executive function and self-regulation was one of the consistently used theoretical models. Social stigma and parental motivation were also used as theoretical models within this dissertation study. Barkley's theory largely influenced the shift from viewing ADHD as simply a behavioral disorder to one with a neuropsychological basis. Social stigma was shown in the research to have a direct influence on parental treatment engagement and efficacy of treatment regimens (Mueller et al., 2012). Parent motivation was influenced by many factors such as how programs are structured, culture, the school system, and stigma (Fabiano, 2007). The literature demonstrated a significant comorbidity among ADHD and other disorders such as Conduct Disorder (CD) and learning disabilities.

The literature varied in types of methods used in examining parental experience with medication however quantitative methods were most often used. In research that explored parental beliefs and perceptions, qualitative studies were widely used. Those studies often involved semi-structured interviews; gathering patterns and meaning of parental responses. The research question of parental experience in seeking treatment is one that begs to be asked. Dreyer, O'Laughlin, Moore, and

Milam (2010) discuss the benefits of understanding parental treatment challenges to assist in assessing and treating those diagnosed with ADHD. It is important to know if the treatment works. However, if we do not understand what the treatment seeking experience was, then we could be losing many parents in their quest for services along the way.

CHAPTER 3. METHODOLOGY

Purpose of the Study

The purpose of this study was to examine the experiences of parents in seeking treatment for their child diagnosed with ADHD. This study takes what has been commonly studied regarding ADHD and a specific type of treatment, and extends that examination into the overall parental experience in seeking treatment. The area of parental experience in seeking treatment was found to be limited within the literature reviewed surrounding this topic. This study used a qualitative case study methodology to acquire a deeper understanding of the experiences parents, of children ages 5-18 years, had in seeking ADHD treatment. A line-by-line and hierarchal data analysis was used to analyze and make interpretations of the verbatim transcriptions of parent participants, researcher field notes, and member checking: the summation from the interviewing phase, demographic surveys, and documents provided by the participants. The data collection and data analysis used in this study will assist the researcher in the examination of the parental experience of seeking treatment for their child diagnosed with ADHD. This qualitative case study approach was used to answer the research question: What are the parental experiences of seeking treatment for their child diagnosed with ADHD?

Research Design

Methodology

This research is considered a multiple-case study as it examined the phenomenon among several parents seeking treatment rather than one parent which would have made it a single-case study (Yin, 2009). The premise of qualitative studies is each participant would have an individual experience with the phenomenon under study, and those individuals' responses can be synthesized among participants to allow for a deeper understanding of the experiences of seeking treatment. The parent participants were encouraged to describe their experiences using semi-structured open-ended questions. The final question allowed for participants to contribute any experiences or information that had not been asked by the researcher. The purpose of this research was the examination and interpretation of the experiences of parents, with the assumption that each parent participant would provide accurate and honest information about their treatment seeking experience.

Sample Type

This researcher used purposeful sampling to obtain 10 parent participants from New York. This allowed parents who met criteria and were available during the time data was collected to be included in this study. The sample was open to both mothers and fathers, but contained only mothers. In one case where a father had inquired of the study, he did not meet inclusionary criteria. The use of purposeful sampling assisted in obtaining meaningful information that aided in answering the research questions. Yin (2009) recommends that a replication containing five, six, or more could demonstrate a strong correlation between the certainty of one's findings. This study could meet those replications with the ten participants and concluded data saturation had been adequately met.

Data Collection Methods and Frequency

All parents participated voluntarily. The data was collected through semi-structured interviews that utilized open-ended questions designed by this researcher. The questions were free flowing and resembled an informal conversation. Interviews were projected to range in duration from 60-90 minutes. The interviews were scheduled for 90 minutes and lasted approximately 28-90 minutes. Upon completion of the interviews, participants were thanked for their participation in this research study and informed that follow-up contact would be made for member checking. Participants were provided with a $20 gift card for their participation in the study. Participants were also provided with a list generated by this researcher of resources where they could obtain information and or assistance with mental health, behavioral needs, and ADHD treatment. Field notes were taken following each session.

Following the interview, both the audio recordings and field notes were transcribed verbatim by this researcher. The participants were coded as Participant 1, Participant 2, etc. The data was backed up in several places and lastly, secured. The data: original audiotapes and original transcriptions were stored in a lockbox at a financial institution. Field notes were also typed, organized, saved, scanned into a computer, and managed in the same fashion as the audiotapes and transcriptions.

Data Analysis Type

The data for this study was analyzed through a line-by-line data analysis performed by this researcher. The research model used was Robert Yin's for a qualitative case study. Yin (2009) discussed five analytic techniques when conducting a case study: pattern matching, explanation building, time series analysis, logic models, and cross-synthesis. A cross-case synthesis was used to analyze the content to the research question. This method allowed for the analysis of multiple-cases of parents to be used to compare and contrast the

findings to obtain themes and meanings. Yin (2009)
recommends several key factors to be used to ensure
a high-quality analysis which were included in this
study: attended to all evidence, addressed possible
rival interpretations, focused on the more significant
components of the case study, and used prior expert
knowledge in the case study. NVivo, qualitative
software, was used to assist with the data reduction
phase. The combination of both approaches allowed
for themes and patterns to be revealed in the data
within a case and between cases. This was a
multiple-case study therefore the cross-case analysis
was equally important to this researcher. Data
analysis was performed over multiple days for each
case as this researcher continuously returned to the
data. Member checking was incorporated to allow
participants the opportunity to review the meaning
that was placed on data and assisted in ensuring the
validity of the findings. Participants could either
confirm the meaning was accurate and/or provide
guidance and correction where it was needed. This
study examined each case in-depth, using multiple
forms of data to obtain themes and patterns.

Credibility

It was important this research maintained the ethical and clinical standards expected in the field of psychology. A concerted effort was made to present each parent's experience accurately as this is especially crucial in qualitative work (Lietz & Zayas, 2010). Credibility was built into this research design through triangulation. The use of multiple theoretical schemes, methods, and data sources is one way this was accomplished (Creswell, 2013). Data triangulation was used in this study where participants provided a variety of data they selected to be reviewed. Some of the data was from school: Individual Education Plan's (IEP), report cards, progress reports, suspension letters, and treatment plans. Other data parents selected to share was from community resources. These documents along with the participant interviews and participant observations consisted of the triangulation of data. Member checking is another way credibility has been maintained in this study. Once the data was transcribed, participants were contacted to check the accuracy of the data analysis ensuring it was reflective of their experiences. Member checking aided in the ability to present the findings in an accurate manner. Audiotapes were discreetly placed during the research session to reduce research reactivity. Biases were discussed with mentor as they presented, attempts to increase self-awareness were employed, and a written journal throughout the research process was maintained. Researcher credibility was established by presenting true and accurate representations of the research findings.

Dependability

Dependability was achieved in this research through several means from procedures and methods to the descriptive information that would allow the reproduction of this study by another researcher. Dependability was further ensured using debriefings with assigned mentor, member checking, and audit trails; all of which helped to ensure dependability (Lietz & Zayas, 2010). An audit trail was used that documented reflexivity. Google Docs was used to assist in documenting and tracking research meetings, researcher decisions, and the reactions of the participants when discussing the coding of transcripts. This study has attempted to establish credibility by including reflexivity, mentor debriefing, audit trails, triangulation, member checking, and rich, thick descriptions.

Target Population and Participant Selection

The larger population from which the sample was drawn was from adult men and women who were parents of a child diagnosed with ADHD. The sample was biological parents of children who had been diagnosed with ADHD. The parents could have been either mothers or fathers however only mothers inquired about the study and/or fathers who did inquire did not meet the criteria to participate. The sample sought treatment services in the past for their child's ADHD symptoms. At the onset of this study, during the recruitment phase, there was not a definitive sample size determined. Instead, there was continued evaluation of the sample size during the data collection process. The projected sample size would be adequate to describe the experience of parents seeking treatment for their children diagnosed with ADHD and therefore answer the research question posed within this study. The sample size was originally projected to be 8 -14 participants or until data saturation was met. In this study the sample included 10 parent participants who each had children diagnosed with ADHD. Recruitment and additional data collection ceased once data saturation was met. Data saturation was evident once the continuous replication of parental experiences was presented in this study.

It is difficult to find a precise recommended case study sample in the literature, however studies that show an increased number of replications containing five, six, or more could be correlated with the certainty of ones' findings (Yin, 2009). Creswell (2013) states that a case study should not exceed four or five cases as that provides more than enough information to identify case themes and perform a cross-case analysis. The recommended sample size in the literature shows considerable ranges while the point of data saturation can be equally argued among researchers. It was agreed data saturation is reached once there is the continuation of replicated findings and the probability of future replications (Mason, 2010). In this small research study, it could be argued data saturation had been met at a faster pace due to the moderate research outcomes than a study with more comprehensive inquiry across disciplines (Charmaz, 2006).

Procedures

Sampling Procedures

The type of sampling strategy used was purposeful sampling. Purposeful sampling was the specific sampling used to obtain research participants. Purposeful sampling allowed this researcher to use participants who were available during the time the data was collected. The accessibility between the researcher and potential parent participants was the hallmark of purposeful sampling (Marshall, 1996). The sampling strategy consisted of recruiting participants through community networks; a local church. Contact was made with the pastor of the church and a request was made for him to allow for the dissemination of information about the research study. This pastor allowed for the distribution of research fliers within his facility. The information encouraged readers to share the fliers with those who may meet the criteria to participate in the study. The information printed on the fliers allowed participants to contact this researcher by calling the phone number listed. Once participants contacted this researcher they were presented with the screening and demographics questions. This was helpful in ascertaining the appropriateness of those interested in participating. The first step was to confirm the biological parental link to the child, followed by the diagnoses being provided by a medical professional. The children were between the ages of 5 and 18 years and lived at home with the parent or parents who were seeking research inclusion. The screening determined the eligibility for the parent. For those parents who met the criteria, a time was scheduled for them to meet to participate in the interview. Before beginning the interview process, the informed consent was presented, reviewed, and written consent was obtained.

Protection of the Participants

There were several ways this researcher sought to protect the participants involved in this study. The initial attempt at participant protection was by having all interested parties, who met the research criteria, sign an informed consent after it was described by this researcher and the participants had the opportunity to read it in full. To maintain anonymity, the names of those involved in the study were coded as Participant 1, Participant 2, etc. There was also a list provided to participants of mental health providers and national organizations that parents could access for mental health and/ or ADHD needs. These were the ways this researcher attempted to protect participants involved in this research study.

Data Collection

In research utilizing case study methodology, the data is often obtained through semi-structured interview questions. This researcher served the dual role of data collector and analyst. Data collection took place in a private office. Once a specified time had been scheduled the researcher met the participant at the designated location. These sessions were held Monday through Sunday from the morning until evening, based on the availability of the participants. Once the participants arrived they were greeted then seated, and the informed consent was reviewed with each participant, and allowances for questions was extended. Once the informed consent had been reviewed, and all questions had been answered, this researcher obtained written consent from the participant. The interview session was described for them before the actual session began. The description explained how the researcher would ask them a set of questions however they were encouraged to add as much detail to their responses as possible. They were advised the sessions would be audio recorded and later transcribed. Sessions were recorded using two audio recorders. The participants were asked to pause or "hold their thought" should the audiotape stop. Once the audio recorder resumed recording, they would be prompted to continue. If they needed a break during our session, participants were encouraged to feel free to inform the researcher. It was stressed these pauses or breaks could be for any reason they see fit. Once participants alerted this researcher of the need for a break, the interview would pause, then resume once the participant was ready to do so. Each participant was thanked for their participation in the study and for the help they were providing the research community as it relates to parental experiences in seeking treatment for ADHD.

Data Analysis

There were various sources of data obtained in the research study to include the recorded interviews, researcher field notes, documents, and information provided by parents during member checking (Creswell, 2007). There was great effort made by the researcher to consider all presented evidence, address rival interpretations, focus on significant case aspects, and use prior expert knowledge (Yin, 2009). The research model used in this study was Robert Yin's data analysis (2009). The data analysis began with this researcher transcribing verbatim the participants' interviews. Once the transcripts were completed they went through the data reduction phase which consisted of the use of NVivo; qualitative data analysis software, and a line-by-line data analysis performed by this researcher. This researcher further looked at the data's patterns and themes and reduced further where needed. Between the two forums, this researcher examined all pertinent categories of data and the emergence of patterns and meaningful incidents (Yin, 2009). The emergence of themes were noted and supported by the content of the interviews. Phrases and concepts were gathered and identified from the interviews and were coded and grouped per recurring themes and sub-themes.

Hierarchal analysis was used to continue to break down the main themes into sub-themes. Each case continued with such probing to inspect for similarities and differences in the single-case and cross-case analysis. This process allowed for generalizations to be made regarding the overall parental experiences in seeking treatment. There were word tables created of each parent case with a uniform framework (Yin, 2009). There were additional word tables created that highlighted other outcomes of interest and processes and allowed for conclusions across cases (Yin, 2009). Cross-case synthesis was then incorporated allowing for the integration of meaning across cases. Each case was summarized relevant to the content provided in the interviews and demographic surveys. The interpretation of the research was then compared/contrasted to the research literature on this subject and concluded with connections being made. The general theme of parental experience in seeking treatment for their children with ADHD and interpretive conclusions were demonstrated by the connection between categories.

Procedures for Presentation of Findings

The NVivo software was used to assist this researcher in the categorization of items that helped to analyze the data more effectively. There were word tables used to display the data from each parent (case); created uniformly (Yin, 2009). Additional word tables were created to demonstrate several findings of interest and processes which aided in the findings of cross-case conclusions (Yin, 2009). During the final phase of conclusions and verification of the data there was an examination of any researcher bias from the onset of the study to its conclusion. The cases were summarized per the information gathered during the interview phase and demographic surveys. This researcher then compared/contrasted the acquired interpretation with the research literature that allowed for several connections to be made. There were general themes of this study and interpretive conclusions were made by the connections between categories.

Researcher Biases

The researcher's bias about this topic involved the interactions between the healthcare industry and parents seeking ADHD treatment. In working with parents of children diagnosed with ADHD in the role of a school social worker from 2004 -2015, some had reported they had not been treated adequately when they sought assistance. Although this has only been reported by a small group of parents, it was a factor this researcher was certain to be aware may have become a bias. One of the ways it was planned to avoid such bias in this research study was to share some of the preliminary findings with the assigned

mentor and other colleagues who may offer

alternative explanations or further data collection may

have been suggested (Yin, 2009). The projected

issue did not arise through the research study as

other areas of the treatment seeking experience took

precedence during participant interviews. Ongoing

journaling was a method used to reduce researcher

bias. Journaling allowed for the examination of any

personal matters, judgments, or research experiences

that may have surfaced and influenced the data

analysis and interpretation, and were later consulted

with assigned mentor to assess for inclusion in the

methodological section of this study (Patton, 2002).

Instruments

Demographic and Screening Questions

When participants called to express interest in

the research study, they were verbally presented with

demographic and screening questions to see if they

met criteria for inclusion. For those parents who

answered "yes" to all questions 1 - 6 they were

eligible for participation in this study. Questions 7 - 11

were demographic questions to gather information on participants' health insurance status, marital status, ethnicity, the highest level of education, and age. Question 12 asked about any documents that the parent had that they may like to share with this researcher at the interview pertaining to their child's ADHD history or treatment. The following is the list of demographic and screening questions used in this study when participants initially called this researcher.

1. Do you have a child between 5-18 years of age?
2. Are you the biological parent of such child with ADHD?
3. Does your child live in the same household as yourself?
4. Is your child currently enrolled in school?
5. Has your child ever been diagnosed with ADHD by a medical professional?
6. Have you ever sought treatment for your child's ADHD diagnosis?
7. Did you have health insurance for your child at the time you sought ADHD treatment?
8. What is your marital status?
9. What is your ethnicity?

10. What is your highest level of education?

11. What is your age?

12. Do you have any of the following documents that you would be interested in sharing: report cards, school progress reports, Individualized Education Plans (IEP), Functional Behavioral Assessments (FBA), and a Behavior Intervention Plan (BIP). Copies of these documents would be brought to the scheduled interview session.

Interviews

The interview guide was the basis for all interviews conducted while combining the informal conversational approach which allowed this researcher to respond immediately to the particulars within each experience described from the interview questions, and the flexibility of personalization between participants (Patton, 2001). The interview method used in this qualitative research methodology was semi-structured interviews utilizing open-ended questions designed by this researcher. The interview guide sought to inquire of participants' experiences of seeking treatment for their child diagnosed with

ADHD. Those experiences crossed social, medical, and educational settings, and research questions attempted to cover such while allowing participants to contribute their own nuances in their search for ADHD treatment. The ability to define the research question could arguably be said to be the most significant step in the research study (Yin, 2009). Without the foundational part of a research study; the research questions, the researcher has the potential to discover later the study lacks the focus and strong direction needed to make any significant conclusions of the data obtained. The following interview questions were used to gain deeper insight into the parental treatment seeking phenomenon:

1. What factors have gone into your decision to seek treatment or not for your child's ADHD diagnosis?
2. What has been your experience with seeking treatment interventions?
3. What have been some of your greatest challenges and or barriers to seeking treatment for your child with ADHD?
4. Have your cultural, religious or other values played in your outlook on treatment for ADHD? If yes, in

what ways?

5. What specific treatment options for ADHD have you been or are you most open to and why?

6. In what way have you felt supported and/or discouraged by your child's school system, in pursuing ADHD treatment?

7. What has been the social, emotional, psychological impact on you regarding treatment seeking since the start of the ADHD symptoms presented until now?

8. What is it like to be a parent trying to navigate systems to get your child treatment for ADHD?

9. What significant experiences stand out for you in regards to seeking treatment for your child?

10. Is there anything that I have not asked that you think would be important for me to know about your ADHD treatment seeking experiences?

Tape Recordings

The use of tape recorders during interviews allowed this researcher to capture the words expressed by participants in response to the research and follow-up questions. There were two recorders used, and they were strategically placed as to not interfere with the flow of the interviews. The use of the recorders later allowed for the interviews to be transcribed verbatim.

Role of the Researcher

In a qualitative study the researcher is the primary instrument and their prior knowledge and experiences assist in the overall effectiveness of conducting such studies. Qualitative studies utilize the human being as the instrument unlike in quantitative studies where the instruments are predominantly questionnaires and tools developed by other researchers (Creswell, 2013; Patton, 2002). In this study the researcher, as the instrument, was responsible for developing the primary research question, all sub questions, conducting participant interviews, making observations of participants, and then interpreting the responses given. The researcher designed semi-structured questions that were more of a conversational flow of engagement over the rigidity found in quantitative methodologies. The skill of the researcher, experiential ability, and thoroughness assisted in building the credibility of this research study (Patton, 2002). Patton (2002) discussed the role of self-awareness during data collection and analysis and how improving self-awareness directly impacts the researcher as the instrument. Reflexivity supported the role of self-awareness by continually bringing the researcher back to a place in their consciousness of questioning their own perspectives. That reflexivity caused the researcher to examine their own perspective on "cultural, political, social, linguistic, and ideological origins" (Patton, 2002, p. 65). The strength in a qualitative study does encompass the level of training and experience of the researcher as well as insightful observations that lend to the overall credibility of the research findings (Patton, 2002). Each individual brings with them their own lens through which all information is processed through; cultural, gender, socio-economic, nationality, etc. This researcher engaged in critical reflexivity to ensure that observations and meanings placed on such were not constrained by the filter held as the researcher in the role of the instrument.

Research Questions and Hypotheses

This research study focused on the parental experiences of seeking treatment for their children diagnosed with attention deficit hyperactivity disorder. The primary research question of the study was: *What is the experience of parents in seeking treatment for their child who is diagnosed with ADHD?* There were no hypotheses in this study as the goal was not to attempt to prove or disprove a theory but rather gain a deeper understanding of the phenomenon as the themes and patterns evolved from the data (Yin, 2009).

Data Analysis

Types of Data to be Analyzed

Data for this research study was collected between July 2015 and November 2015. The data was collected from multiple sources, consisting of recorded participant interviews, researcher field notes were taken after each interview, documents presented by the parents, as well as the parent feedback provided during the member checking phase (Creswell, 2007). Qualitative data can be analyzed through several models (Creswell, 2009). One way this researcher ensured a high-quality analysis was by attending the evidence presented, addressing possible rival interpretations of the data, focusing on significant aspects of the case, and use of prior expert knowledge (Yin, 2009). This study used a line-by-line analysis for data analysis as discussed by Robert Yin (2009). The line-by-line analysis reviews the transcripts by reading each line while making notations to any significant information contained therein. The researcher looked for patterns and themes within and between cases in this study.

Preparation of Data for Analysis

The data analysis began with this researcher transcribing verbatim the participants' interviews. The data was transcribed by this researcher listening to the recorded interviews and typing the content into a Microsoft Word document. Completed transcripts were printed out in full and contained a master copy and a working copy. The field notes were transcribed verbatim after each interview session by this researcher by looking at the written content and typing it into a Microsoft Word document. The documents were reviewed by this researcher and notes were made, and the text was highlighted regarding significant data. Member checking was performed by discussing interview content and meaning with participants to confirm the accuracy and correct meaning of patterns and themes that developed.

Actual Analyses to be Carried Out

Once the transcripts were completed they went through the data reduction phase which consisted of the use of NVivo; qualitative data analysis software, and a line-by-line data analysis performed by this researcher. Between the two forums, this researcher examined all pertinent categories of data and the emergence of patterns and meaningful incidents (Yin, 2009). The emergence of themes were noted and supported by the content of the interviews. Each case continued with such probing. Cross-case synthesis was then incorporated allowing for the integration of meaning across cases. A word table was used to display data from each case. Hierarchal analysis was used to continue to break down the main themes into sub-themes. Finally, data was examined for similarities and differences using a case analysis and cross-case analysis that allowed for generalizations of the overall parental experiences in seeking treatment. Field notes were analyzed by looking for significant patterns and themes within and across cases. The notes were reviewed using the same line-by-line data analysis that was used for the transcripts. The documents were reviewed for any additional value they add to understanding the parental experience in seeking treatment for their child's ADHD.

Storage and Protection of Data

Following the interview, both the audio recordings and field notes were later transcribed verbatim by this researcher. The participants were coded as Participant 1, Participant 2, etc. The data was backed up in several places and lastly, secured. The place where the data was backed up was on a computer and flash drive. Only this researcher has access to each. The data on the computer was secured through password protection. The flash drive, original audiotapes, and original transcriptions were maintained in a financial institution's lock box upon completion of the study. Field notes were also typed, organized, saved, scanned into a computer, and managed in the same fashion as the audio-tapes and transcriptions. For example, coding or removal of identifiers as soon as possible, limitation of access to data, use of locked file cabinets, protection of computer-based data systems, etc. were all employed to store and protect the research data.

Ethical Considerations

Institutional Review Board

This research study was submitted to and received full approval to conduct research from Capella University Institutional Review Board (IRB). The information contained in the research proposal was accurate, and all research duties were aligned with the original research plan and application to conduct such research.

Informed Consent to Research

All participants were provided with a written informed consent before the commencement of the research interviews. Participants were not coerced into participation and each signed prior to beginning engagement in this research study. The American Psychiatric Association (2002) outlines the parameters of the informed consent and each aspect that must be contained therein. Those aspects were included in the informed consent used by the researcher and approved by the IRB. The purpose of the study as it relates to parental experience in seeking treatment for their children diagnosed with ADHD was explained. Parents were advised the projected duration would be between 60-90 minutes in length and the process of such interview was detailed. Participants were advised they were free to cease their involvement at any time and for any reason should they feel uncomfortable with continuing and there were no consequences to them for their decision. Potential participant's risks for engagement in this study were assessed and there were found to be no risks in participating. It was explained that there were no personal benefits to the participant but rather the larger research community could possibly benefit from the research findings. The limits of confidentiality were discussed and included in the informed consent that pertained to disclosures of child or vulnerable adult abuse, the participants' plans to harm themselves, others, or commit suicide. Participants were advised they would receive a small token of appreciation for their participation; a $20 Visa gift card. The names and contact information of the researcher and dissertation mentor were provided to each participant where they could direct any questions and inquire about research participant's rights.

Recording Voices

In this research study, a signed informed consent was required prior to engaging participants in audio recordings. The request to engage participants in audio recordings was made in the informed consent. All participants had the opportunity to read, ask questions, and sign the informed consent in two places: signifying their participation in the study and agreement to be audiotaped. The purpose of audio taping was explained to the participants prior to beginning to record the interview session.

Confidentiality

Maintaining anonymity for participants was of key importance during all phases of this study. Parents were assured that their names or any other identifiable information, would not be used in any text and extensive measures would be taken to protect their identity. Parents were ascribed codes of Participant 1, Participant 2, and Participant 3, etc. Measures to ensure confidentiality were taken by storing all data appropriately; limitations to access of data, password protected files on the computer, locked filing cabinet, the use of coding, and removing personal identifiers as soon as possible. Upon completion of this study, all data was backed up and will be stored as previously stated, for a minimum of seven years.

Debriefing Standards

As a method to enhance the trustworthiness of the research design, member checking was incorporated. This process allowed the participants to receive information about the preliminary results of the study and correct any misunderstanding or errors that may have been made by this researcher. That provided the researcher the opportunity to correct those preliminary findings before research conclusions were made.

Expected Findings

The researcher expected findings would be a deeper understanding of parental experiences of seeking treatment for their children diagnosed with ADHD. Although parent participants differed in demographics such as age, culture, and other factors, there were expectations regarding themes and patterns. It was anticipated that patterns would be presented in this qualitative study and common themes among participants would possibly be found. It was also expected that participants would be able to adequately recall their experiences of seeking treatment and provide an honest account of those experiences. A qualitative study seeks to gain deeper insight and meaning into the phenomenon under study. The data uncovered through this qualitative study directed the conclusions of such research rather than the researcher having a preconceived notion of the projected research outcomes. The main goal of this study was to understand the experiences of parents as they pursued treatment for their children diagnosed with ADHD. The individual perspectives and meanings were used to gather overarching themes and patterns. Throughout this study this researcher had to be aware of assumptions and researcher bias and use the aforementioned steps to address them as they arose. A deeper understanding of parental experiences, the ability to recall and provide truthful accounts, and the belief that patterns and common themes would be present, were the central expected findings this researcher had about this study.

CHAPTER 4. DATA COLLECTION AND ANALYSIS

Introduction: The Study and the Researcher

Chapter 4 will focus on the discussion relative to the data that was collected and analyzed from the ten parent participants who described their experiences of seeking treatment for their children who were diagnosed with ADHD. The main research question in this study is "What is the experience of parents in seeking treatment for their child who is diagnosed with attention deficit hyperactivity disorder?" This qualitative study used Robert Yin's (2009) case study research model. Each parent participant was interviewed and those interviews were later transcribed and analyzed using a within-case analysis. Upon completion of analyzing the 10 interviews, a cross-case synthesis of all cases was performed. This allowed for the multiple-cases of parents to be used to compare and contrast the findings to obtain the themes and meanings to be presented in this chapter.

The study analysis provided pertinent categories of data and the emergence of patterns and meaningful incidents (Yin, 2009). The emergence of themes were noted by this researcher and supported by the content of the interviews. A cross-case synthesis was performed that allowed for the ability to integrate meaning across multiple-cases. A word table was used for displaying data from each case. The main themes were further broken down into sub-themes using hierarchal analysis. Data was finally examined for similarities and differences by using case analysis and cross-case analysis that presented generalizations of parental experiences in seeking treatment. Field notes were also included for analysis and all documents were reviewed for significant occurrences or value they added to understanding the parental experience in treatment seeking.

The discussion in Chapter four will include the researcher's interest in the ADHD treatment seeking phenomenon and the researcher's background and experience in conducting the qualitative research approach. Further discussion will include the role of the researcher as it pertains to data collection and analysis as well as any possible researcher effects on the data at any stage throughout the research process.

There is a description included of the demographics of parent participants which were collected during initial contact when parents called to inquire about the study. Those descriptions will include the age of a child diagnosed with ADHD, medical insurance status at time of treatment seeking, parent's: marital status, ethnicity, educational status, and age. All participants were asked if they had any documents they would like to share with this researcher such as: report cards, school progress reports, Individualized Education Plans (IEP), Functional Behavioral Assessments (FBA), or Behavior Intervention Plans (BIP). They were asked to bring any such items they would like to share to the scheduled interview session.

The research methodology used in this study was discussed next and included a description of the multiple-case study methodology, the research setting, and the type of interview utilized. The procedures used in conducting the 10 interviews were described. The data presentation and data analysis results were presented through a description of the emerging themes and meaning's that evolved through the expressed experiences of the participants. Such experiences were captured in their own words using direct quotes. The data analysis contained the single-case analysis then moves along to capture the multiple-case syntheses. There was a brief overview of what the interpretation stage would consist of, however; an in-depth discussion of such was included in full detail in Chapter 5. This chapter concluded with a summary of the research findings.

The Researcher's Interests in the Phenomenon

This researcher is an African American female student pursuing a PhD in General Psychology at Capella University with an interest in understanding the experiences of parents who seek treatment for their children who have been diagnosed with ADHD. The researcher is a licensed social worker and worked for 11 years as a school social worker in a public-school setting. In this capacity, there have been many students with ADHD who have been treated by the researcher in the role of the social worker through counseling, consulting, and crisis intervention. There were parents who have sought treatment and shared some of those experiences. In other cases, parents began their quest for treatment and never followed through and those reasons for the lack of follow through were not always communicated. There were student success stories for children who obtained the right treatment that matched their symptoms and parent preferences for treatment options. When treatment was successful, it positively impacted the student's overall school success and social functioning. It was the interest of this researcher to find out what the experience was like for parents as they sought treatment with the hopes of building upon those successful outcomes and addressing the challenges others may have faced. With this interest in mind, the research question emerged: What is the experience of parents in seeking treatment for their child who is diagnosed with attention deficit hyperactivity disorder?

Researcher's Background, Training, and Experience in Conducting the Research Approach

This researcher is a Licensed Master Social Worker (LMSW), who has extensive experience working with children with ADHD. Being employed as a school social worker from 2004-2015 has allowed for ongoing interactions with children and parents regarding such diagnosis. This researcher currently works in the field of social work where clinical observations and interviewing client populations are an expected part of the job requirement. This researcher has extensive experience in conducting interviews with children, adolescents, and adults from school social work, forensic, psychiatric, and community counseling settings. In the most recent work setting, this researcher was responsible for interviewing students, parents, and teachers for matters related to significant school events. In some cases, those interviews were related to the New York State Dignity for All Students Act (DASA) where a report of bullying behavior was being initiated, or a follow-up inquiry was made.

The researcher has extensive experience with hundreds of children diagnosed with ADHD in the capacity of counseling services, crisis intervention, and providing supportive services to parents and educators. This direct experience with this population assisted in an understanding of the etiology of the disorder, and some of the common research-based treatment modalities. It also provided an awareness of social stigma commonly attached to the disorder and this knowledge was used to normalize parents' feelings and provide a supportive setting where they felt comfortable to share their stories.

This researcher is a graduate student at Capella University with a major in General Psychology. Some of the coursework achieved through Capella University has included such courses as Qualitative Analysis and Advanced Qualitative Analysis. The research courses presented throughout the Track I, II, and III Capella Colloquiums provided additional learning experiences. Throughout the process of data collection and analysis, the researcher continued to return to the data to ensure interviews and data analysis were accurate representations of the presumed meanings communicated by the participants. The researcher also participated in member checking, which included contacting participants to confirm if the ascribed meaning was accurate and if not to correct such meanings placed on the presenting data. The researcher continued to become knowledgeable about the case study methodology by reading research articles about case studies and those which have used case studies, dissertations having used case studies, and the Yin text. Finally, any personal matters, judgments, or experiences which could have influenced the data analysis and interpretation process, was discussed and consulted with the researcher's assigned mentor and assessed for inclusion in the methodological section of the research study (Patton, 2002).

Some key qualities needed by the researcher during the interviews were: good listening skills, adaptability, and flexibility, asking good questions, having a firm grasp of the issues being studied and avoiding bias (Yin, 2009). This researcher needed to listen to the audible responses of the participants, but take in the non-verbal signs of communication present. This researcher observed the congruency between the verbal responses and the physical reactions in the facial and body language. This researcher was flexible to those things that may have caused both minor and major shifts in the research design while keeping the original purpose of the research at the heart of the focus (Yin, 2009).

Role of the Researcher Played in Data Collection and Analysis

The researcher became the primary instrument in this qualitative study, and prior knowledge and experiences helped in conducting an effective case study inquiry. The research questions, participant interviews, observations, and interpretations were all performed by the researcher. The semi-structured questions were designed to have a conversational flow between participant and researcher. Some of the factors assisting in building credibility in this research design were the researcher's skills, experience, and thoroughness (Patton, 2002). Self-awareness and reflexivity also aided the researcher as an instrument. The researcher engaged in reflexivity by constantly questioning one's own perspectives. Insightful observations and previous training and experience contributed to the strength of this study (Patton, 2002). Critical reflexivity was employed during observations and the formulation of themes and meanings placed on data to ensure one's own perspectives were not driving the research outcomes.

Researcher Effects on the Data

There are ways in which a researcher could affect the data and in this case, it could have been affected if researcher bias was included in the data collection or analysis. One of the stated researcher biases was some parents had informed the researcher in her professional capacity they had difficulty obtaining ADHD treatment because of their interactions with medical providers. This researcher was very aware this could be a potential bias and previously discussed that in the dissertation. The data did not support this previously held belief and shifted towards other trends in the experience of treatment seeking. Had the data supported this belief it would have been important for this researcher to use all of the safeguards already implemented in this study:

reflexivity, member checking, consulting with a mentor, field notes to include reflections of thoughts and feelings towards the process and developing themes and patterns. This topic is a professional one that this researcher has worked with many times from children diagnosed and parents seeking treatment services. This research has the potential to be a great benefit to treatment providers so they have a greater understanding of the experience of parents seeking treatment for their children diagnosed with ADHD.

Description of the Sample (Participants)

The Participants

The population for this research study included ten mothers who have sought treatment for their children who have been diagnosed with ADHD. The participants received information about the study directly from the church that agreed to assist with recruitment by posting flyers, making announcements at church, and disseminating information. Information was also obtained from people that participants know who received it and passed the information along. Each participant called the researcher at the phone number listed on the flyer and a phone interview was conducted. During the phone interview, this researcher was assessing to ensure the participants met the criteria to be included in this research study. It was also an opportunity to explain to the prospective participant what the study was about, and what the process would be if they met the criteria, and agreed to participate.

Purposeful sampling was used in this study which assisted in gaining insight into the phenomenon of parental treatment seeking by obtaining "information rich" experiences from the participants (Patton, p.40, 2002). A purposeful sampling was used to allow parents to be included in the study who met criteria and were available to participate during the data collection phase. The researcher sought to include participants who could answer the research question being asked and contribute to the knowledge of the phenomenon under study in a meaningful way. Data saturation occurs once there is a continuation of replications of the research findings or there is the probability that there will be future replications (Mason, 2010). The data was saturated with the ninth participant but a tenth participant was included to ensure that data saturation was met.

The inclusionary factors consisted of (a) parents who have a child between 5 - 18 years of age; (b) the parent was the biological parent of the child; (c) the child lives in the home of the parent; (d) the child is enrolled in school; (e) the child has been diagnosed with ADHD by a medical professional and; (f) the parent has sought treatment for their child's ADHD diagnosis. The study did not preclude any race/ethnicity or gender of the parents or their children. Upon determination that the criteria were met by the participant and the phone interview was completed, an interview date and time was coordinated with the participant to meet at a private professional office. All participants' identities were protected by the assignment of pseudonyms such as Participant One, Participant Two, Participant Three, etc.

The ages of the participants ranged from 28-51 years of age. There was one participant in her twenties, one in her thirties, seven in their forties, and one in her fifties. The marital statuses of the parent participants were two single, five married, two divorced, and one separated. All ten participants had health insurance for their children at the time they sought treatment services for ADHD. There were nine participants that identified their ethnicity as Caucasian, and one participant who identified herself as Caucasian, Italian, Russian, and Hungarian. The participants had a range of educational experience with four reporting some college, two with Associates, three with Bachelors, and one with a Master's degree. All participants stated during the phone interview they had a document/s they would be willing to share with this researcher at the scheduled interview. All 10 participants live within the same county in New York State.

The Description of the Participants

Participant One

Participant One was 28 years old, single, and has one son. She identified her ethnicity as Caucasian. She has an Associate's degree and worked in the medical field. Her eight-year-old son had been diagnosed by his pediatrician with ADHD-Combined Type with Hyperactivity and Inattention. He received the diagnosis of ADHD at five-years of age. She reported her son having difficulty in school dating back to pre-kindergarten. Her son was in fourth grade, had a 504 Accommodation previously, and had an IEP since third grade. There were several school difficulties which included suspensions, referrals to specialized behavioral programs, and being asked by the principal to keep her son home for a period of two weeks. The continued behavioral difficulties in the school setting led the participant to seek treatment. At the time, she chose to seek treatment she did have medical insurance for her son. The participant was soft spoken, clear in presenting her experiences and thoughts on ADHD. She was forthcoming and became emotional in discussing some parts of her story, in particular how her son has been affected by the symptoms of ADHD. She described an experience where she was called by the principal and told to keep her son home for two weeks due to his aggressive behaviors. The participant further shared she was not offered a 504, or any suggestions for mediating the problem. She spoke in a shaken voice of how she was not offered anything until the next school year when she advocated on behalf of her son the first day of school. The participant had sought multiple sources of treatment: pediatrician, school-based services (504 Accommodation), supports, counseling, IEP), outside counseling with a therapist, psychiatrist, change in diet with Feingold's food diet, and medication management which consisted of six different medications. The participant concluded they had an appointment to return to the doctor as the medication is no longer working and she believes there is something more going on with her son than just the ADHD.

Participant Two

Participant Two was a 43 years old, married, mother of four children. She identifies her ethnicity as Caucasian. She had a Bachelor's degree and worked as a teaching assistant in a public school in a special education classroom. Her nine-year-old daughter had been diagnosed by a medical doctor with ADHD-Combined Type with Hyperactivity and Inattention. She received the diagnosis of ADHD at six years of age. She was diagnosed with Autism Spectrum Disorder (ASD) and Anxiety Disorder (AD). She had a

504 Accommodation and the participant plans to seek for a full evaluation for consideration of special education classification due to some current educational challenges. The participant reported her husband was considered to have a learning disability when he was in school. She had a son diagnosed with autism. The parents did not initially agree on pursuing medication with the mother wanting to probe the concerns further and the father being more reserved. As the social and academic difficulties increased the mother was able to express her concerns again to the father who was later agreeable on the decision to seek treatment. At the time, they chose to seek treatment they did have medical insurance in place for their daughter. The participant was relaxed yet eager to share her story, the whole story inclusive of all the nuances that go along with the ADHD symptomology. The participant spoke about the great difficulty in receiving direction and resources from professionals to help her daughter. She has spent much time researching the disorder and suggested strategies to mediate the symptoms. She felt the schools should have something to provide the parents of where they can go and resources that

will help their children. Despite having a 504 Accommodation the participant reports there have been times where the accommodations were not followed. She taught her daughter how to advocate for herself during these times. Advocating for services played an important role in this participant's experience. The cost of not having an advocate or not advocating for herself often meant not receiving the supportive services her child needed to be successful. As we concluded the interview, she shared her deep concerns for her daughter as she moved to the middle school next year and questioned how will she function in that environment? She planned to begin the steps now to having her evaluated with the hopes of moving her into a special education program similar to the classroom she works in. The participant had sought a number of sources for treatment: pediatrician, neurologist, behavioral specialist, psychiatrist, therapist, Early Intervention Services (speech and occupational therapy), medication management, and school-based services (IEP, 504 Accommodation, school-based counseling, occupational therapy, and speech therapy).

Participant Three

Participant Three was 42 years old, divorced, and has one son. She identified her ethnicity as Caucasian. She reported having some college education and worked in medical billing. Her son is 16 years old and in the twelfth grade. He was diagnosed with ADHD Combined Type at approximately seven-years old and began a medication treatment regimen at eight. The participant said she sought treatment on her own after her son struggled academically for several years. She said the poignant occurrence to seeking treatment was a discussion with the teacher who suggested she seek medication for her son "now" so he would not struggle in 4th grade, since it would be more difficult. There was a family history of ADHD with the participant reporting she had undiagnosed symptoms of ADHD and continued to struggle with such symptoms in adulthood. There was also a maternal uncle and the child's half-brother through his father, who had been diagnosed. The parents were separated at the time that treatment was sought, however they both agreed to seek treatment, which included medication management. There was medical insurance in place at the time of treatment seeking. The participant was reserved in her responses as we began, but as she became more comfortable, she was able to open up more as evidenced in the length of her responses to the questions. The participant spoke about the difficult decision she faced when choosing medication to treat her son's ADHD. She was able to move past her reluctance and stigma of medication and spoke about how she came to a place of accepting it once she saw the positive results in her son's behavior and received feedback from his teachers. She stopped providing the medication to her son over the summer and he later reported side effects once the medication resumed. At that point, the participant ceased administering the medication. At the time of the interview, he was not on medication for ADHD. Although she gave high praise for some of the teachers who helped along the way, she stated the school was the most difficult part of her journey. There were issues with the 504 not being implemented, being terminated prematurely, and some teachers who were not helpful in seeing her son succeed. The participant had sought treatment through several forums: school-based treatment with a 504 Accommodation, counseling with the school psychologist, over-the-counter herbal remedies, food restrictions of red dye number 40, preservatives and other food dyes, the pediatrician, psychologist, and medication management (multiple medications and several rounds of titrated medications).

Participant Four

Participant Four was a 43 year old, married, mother of two children. She identified her ethnicity as Caucasian. Participant Four had a Bachelor's degree and worked for a bus company that transported students with a special education classification. Her oldest of two children is a boy, age 16, in tenth grade, who had been diagnosed by a pediatrician with ADHD. He was diagnosed in the third grade at approximately eight-years old. The participant sought treatment at that time for behavioral challenges he was having in school. He accepted a mood stabilizer medication as prescribed by his psychiatrist, and has depression. In earlier evaluations they considered, then ruled out, Asperger's and a learning disability.

There were family members with ADHD symptoms including a maternal uncle and maternal great-grandfather. At the time treatment was sought, the parents were in agreement about the pursuit of treatment and later the treatment recommendations. There was medical insurance in place at the time they sought treatment. However, the participant chose to pay for treatment when they found a provider who did not accept insurance. They eventually had to terminate with that provider because they could no longer afford the policy. The participant was soft spoken, forthcoming with her thoughts and experiences. The participant spoke about the multiple providers she sought for her son's treatment. Those many referrals were a source of stress as she followed up with one and was then referred to another. Each provider posed their own set of challenges. She did have favorable remarks about the pediatrician experience that they were thorough, easy to work with, and explained about ADHD. The participant described the pediatrician as being limited in his scope of practice as her son got older, and a referral was made to see a psychiatrist who would perfom a more comprehensive evaluation. The mother also spoke about her school experience and the lack of direction and resources that were provided. She felt the school should have known there were concerns with her son given the time they interacted with him and she believed they were not permitted to give parents information about supports such as a 504 Accommodation, because they do not want to incur the cost. The participant also spoke favorably about her experience with the psychologist and that coupled with medication was the specific treatments she was most open to. The participant had sought multiple treatment options to include a pediatrician, psychiatrist, therapists, psychiatric and educational evaluations, psychologists, counseling through the Employee Assistance Program (EAP), natural homeopathic, restricted foods, change of diet, and medication management.

Participant Five

Participant Five was a 45 year old, married, mother of three children. She identified her ethnicity as Caucasian. She had some college and was currently on disability. Her youngest of three sons, age 13, has been diagnosed by a neurologist with ADHD. He was diagnosed within the last 90 days. The participant had sought treatment for the symptoms over the years and was told by teachers, school psychologist, neurologist, and pediatrician there was nothing wrong with her son. Treatment was sought after continued lack of school success that resulted in two times being retained before reaching the sixth grade. The participant went to the school for assistance, and they referred her to her pediatrician, who referred her to a neurologist for further testing. The neurologist diagnosed her son with ADHD, learning and processing weaknesses, reading fluency issues, and auditory and executive processing weaknesses. It was further noted the child has poor math skills and is below average in reading. This doctor concluded by recommending a 504 Accommodation. There is a half-brother noted as being diagnosed with ADHD. There was marital disagreement discussed responding to the ADHD symptoms and if their son had ADHD. The mother expressed her reluctance in believing her son has the disorder. There was insurance at the time treatment was sought. The participant was forthcoming in the interview. She was able to elaborate at length about her experiences regarding seeking treatment. There were several occasions where she did tear up and/or begin crying as she described the difficulty of trying to get her son treatment, not wanting him to be diagnosed with ADHD, and trying to help him academically. She spoke about the many times she asked the school for help for her son and not receiving a response, feeling like she was a burden, and feeling the school did not care about her son. She was provided a 504 Accommodation, but describes it as not being implemented. She sought an evaluation for special education classification and was told her son did not qualify. The participant sought treatment from the pediatrician, neurologist, therapist, medication management, school system 504 Accommodation, special education evaluation, and tutoring.

Participant Six

Participant Six was a 43 year old, single mother of two children. She identified her ethnicity as Caucasian. She had some college. Her youngest son,

age 11, had been diagnosed with ADHD by a
neurologist. He was diagnosed at approximately
three-years old shortly after the participant sought
treatment for concerns she had regarding his
behaviors at pre-school, hyperactivity, and engaging
in dangerous conduct such as running towards a road
before being stopped. There were no diagnosed
comorbidities according to the parent. The participant
reported the child's father has observable symptoms
of ADHD. When the participant sought treatment, she
reported she and the child's father had severed their
relationship, therefore, she was the primary party
responsible for the type of care, if any, her son would
receive. She did have insurance for her son at the
time she sought treatment. The participant was able
to be engaged although needed prompting to
elaborate on the information shared. She spoke about
the limited social supports she has and difficulty in
making the decision to treat her son with medication.
There was some social strain within her familial
relationships (parents and sister) as a result of this
decision as they did not agree on the use of ADHD
medication. There were some negative effects of the
medication which made her son like a 'zombie' –

corrected through a medication change. There were
issues of not feeling heard when working with the
initial neurologist. The participant sought a second
neurologist of which she was then pleased with the
level of communication and attention given to her son.
The role of the pediatrician appeared to be limited
except for facilitating the parent's referral request to
the neurologist. There were challenges with school-
based treatment, in particular, the 504
Accommodation not being followed. The testing
modifications were not being implemented and the
student struggled nightly with homework, however,
homework was not addressed through the 504. The
participant sought treatment from the pediatrician who
provided a referral to a neurologist. She saw two
neurologists and continues with the second one at the
time of the interview. They engaged in play therapy,
school-based treatment to include a 504
Accommodation, and medication management. They
found the medication to be successful in treating the
ADHD symptoms.

Participant Seven

Participant Seven was a 49 year old, divorced, mother of three children. She identified her ethnicity as Caucasian. She had some college. Her youngest of three children, age 12, had been diagnosed with ADHD. He was evaluated at three-years old for speech services which he was found eligible. He was placed on Focalin by a neurologist for behavioral issues in kindergarten but did not receive a diagnosis of ADHD at that time. The participant sought treatment for her son for significant behavioral issues while in daycare when he was asked to leave several programs and a summer camp. The behaviors were present in kindergarten resulting in suspensions and many phone calls home and continued through 1st and 2nd grade when he was removed from his local school district and placed in a specialized program outside the district. Some of the early diagnoses her son received were Autism Spectrum Disorder, anxiety, ODD, then later in fourth grade; ADHD. The mother reported she has observable signs of adult ADHD. The father lives locally, but it was the participant's responsibility for deciding to seek and accept any treatment options. She did have insurance for her son at the time she sought treatment. The participant was comfortable and open in telling her experience. With the first question and throughout she was eager to share her story including as many components as she could remember. She discussed the difficulty her son had in school, questioned how it was her son was with professionals and seen by so many professionals, yet nobody told her that her son had ADHD until 4th grade. You could hear the change in her voice as she described being blamed by professionals for her son's behavior and being told by her parents he needed a spanking. The participant described, "that moment," when she knew she would have to make the hardest decision — to have her son hospitalized. She described the painful decision, but yet knowing she had to do it. Two years previously the participant found and became involved in supportive community programs that have greatly helped. While supports have helped, she stated there were few supports for the child who has ADHD. The participant sought numerous providers in a quest for treatment for her son's ADHD symptoms: pediatrician, neurologist, psychiatrists, multiple therapists, hospitalizations, medication management, an emergency care service that brings therapists to your location, and school-based treatment; speech services, specialized programs and components outlined in an IEP.

Participant Eight

Participant Eight is 51 years old, married, and had three children. She identified her ethnicity as Caucasian, Italian, Russian, and Hungarian. She had a Master's degree in Social Work and was a licensed clinical social worker who worked with children with behavioral and mental health disorders. She had extensive experience in working with children and specific experience with ADHD. She felt her professional knowledge and experience helped her in understanding the symptoms her child presented and enabled informed treatment decisions. The participant's oldest son is 13-years old and had been diagnosed by a medical professional with ADHD Inattentive Type between second and third grade. He did not have an IEP or 504 Accommodation and there was no history of behavioral concerns presented at school. This son received a diagnosis of sleep apnea about one year following the ADHD diagnosis; the participant questioned how much of the sleep apnea diagnosis influenced the ADHD symptoms. The participant had observed the same ADHD characteristics in her husband that her son presented, although her husband did not have a formal diagnosis. The parents did not initially agree on pursuing treatment or later agree on the course of treatment for the ADHD symptoms. At the time, they chose to seek treatment they had medical insurance for their son. After the son's continued academic difficulties, the husband later agreed to a medication treatment course recommended by the family pediatrician. The participant appeared to be at ease with sharing; her responses were thought out and articulated clearly and completely. She was forthcoming and easy to engage during this interview. The participant described positive experiences in her pursuit for treatment that included the pediatrician, the school system, and medication. There was a time when the parents inquired with the school about a 504 Accommodation and were told it was not necessary.

The teachers were providing several academic modifications to assist in student success. The parents did eventually come to an agreement regarding the pursuit of treatment and how they came to that resolution in the interview. After the interview, she discussed her desire to follow-up with her son regarding the sleep apnea to see if those symptoms are presenting themselves again as he recently was asking her questions about his past related treatment. As the interview session ended the participant expressed she hoped the information shared would be helpful to the research study. The participant spoke about her decision to seek treatment from the family pediatrician. She stated it was the pediatrician who prescribed the medication for the ADHD symptoms. The participant pondered if seeking a specialist would have been the better route. This issue was resolved with the success they have had in controlling the ADHD symptoms through the treatment regimen recommended by the pediatrician.

Participant Nine

Participant Nine is a 47-year old woman, who was married with three children. She identifies her ethnicity as Caucasian. She had a Bachelor's degree in Nursing and worked as a school nurse. In her professional capacity, she worked with many children and families who have ADHD and worked to provide those families with resources (she felt she did not have) as they started on their path for treatment. The participant's son is the second born of three children, and he is 11 years old and was in the sixth grade. He had been diagnosed with ODD, ADHD, Pandas, Sensory Processing Disorder, Tourette's Disorder, and assessed for possible Asperger's Disorder. There were behavioral concerns as early as two-years old and school suspensions at age five (in kindergarten). The parents sought treatment from their pediatrician as a result of the behavioral challenges. There were challenges discussed in seeking treatment with the pediatrician; not receiving a clear diagnosis, lack of follow-up calls, and later receiving an angry call from the pediatrician because the family sought a second opinion. The participant described herself as having ADHD symptoms along with OCD. She stated her husband had been described as being hyper during his childhood, although he was now described as being 'laid back.' The parents were not initially in agreement in pursuing treatment, acceptance of the diagnosis of ADHD, nor the recommend treatment via medication management. This conflict became a point of contention within the marriage, nearly causing separation. The couple came to an agreement to treat the ADHD symptoms with medication and to complement the other treatments to reduce such symptoms. There was insurance at the time they sought treatment for their son. The participant was eager to share her story. She was forthcoming, needed little prompting, and was easy to engage. The participant spoke at length about the difficulties presented in accessing school-based treatment, the stigma associated with ADHD, and the lack of information and resources available within her community. She discussed how stigma was preventing her husband from accepting the ADHD diagnosis and how she was able to come to a resolve the condition. She was later able to convey her resolutions to her husband that he became agreeable to support medication treatment. A shared experience were remarks described by her son's teacher advising her 'special education' kids were not always as successful as mainstream students. This verbalized belief from a teacher is the sentiment this participant received from the school system; that she should not expect success for her son because he is one of 'those kids.' The participant further expressed hopes for her child to find his own success; being able to work, be happy, and be a contributing member of society. She had sought numerous treatment modalities for her son: pediatric, neurologist, exercise, change in diet, homeopathic, extracurricular activities, different medications for ADHD, and school-based; 504 Accommodation, IEP, school counseling, and special transportation.

Participant Ten

Participant Ten is a 39-year-old woman, separated from her husband with whom she shared custody, and had one daughter. She identified her ethnicity as Caucasian and had an Associate's

Degree. She worked full time and had extensive volunteer experience in schools and in her community. The participant's daughter was nine-years old, in the fourth grade, and had been diagnosed with ADHD and anxiety. Her daughter received Early Intervention Services in pre-kindergarten under an IEP, which was terminated prior to entering kindergarten. Upon entry into kindergarten, the child was eligible for a 504 Accommodation, which continued at the time of the research interview. The participant reported being diagnosed herself with ADHD when she was 16 years old and struggled through most of her school age years, but 'she made it.' The parents did not initially agree on seeking treatment whereas the father felt she would grow out of it. With firsthand experience of what it was like to live with ADHD, the mother persisted on seeking treatment services for her daughter. The participant appeared to be at ease in the interview and answered with a soft-spoken voice that began to shake when discussing her child's limited social connectedness within her peer relationships. The participant spoke about her own research and coming to school meetings 'ready to fight' to get her daughter the accommodations needed. Oftentimes, staff would suggest removing items from the 504 which were essential pieces of her daughter's success. The participant had to advocate for those items to remain in the 504. The overall experience with the 504 expressed was that it was often not followed. The participant had to contact the social worker listed on the 504 to provide mandated counseling and the social worker said she was not aware of such. The mother had to repeat the follow up because after mandated 504 services started, the counselor was only seeing the child in group counseling, when the group and individual counseling was listed on the 504. The participant had to contact both classroom teachers whom each said they were not aware of the 504 and did not provide the testing accommodations as outlined within the 504. The participant become upset during the interview as she described the social impact of ADHD and her daughter's peer relationships. She expressed her daughter has not found any connections within the group of kids she was with for three years and did not have a best friend. The participant remarked about sharing her daughter with her dad, and how the participant does not feel like her daughter fits in. Through tears, the participant went on to describe how she asked her daughter who she sits with at lunch. The daughter describes sitting next to people, but not speaking with them. The participant sought treatment from their pediatrician, pediatric neurologist, school social worker, outside counseling services, school-based accommodations and supports, a 504 Accommodation, and most recently a psychiatric evaluation. Extracurricular activities were organized by the participant to keep the child active and socially involved with her peers.

Research Methodology Applied to the Data Analysis

The methodology used in this multiple-case study was Yin (2009). The 10 research participants were interviewed over a five-month period and interviews were held at a private professional office. All interviews were performed as scheduled at the time of the initial phone interview, and participants all arrived within 10 minutes of the scheduled time. An 11th parent (father), called to inquire about the study, but his child did not have a of ADHD diagnosis.

Within this professional office, there was privacy for participants. An additional step to maintain privacy was to schedule participants with enough space between appointments so there would not be an overlap of the time one arrived and the other left. During each interview the setting provided adequate lighting, quiet surroundings, the participant was made comfortable by the selection of chairs used, bottles of water provided, and confidentiality upheld throughout each session.

There were two digital audio recorders used for every interview. The recorders were discreetly placed after consent was provided, so they would not be a distraction to the interviewing process. The 10 participant interviews were transcribed by this researcher who allowed for the assurance that each word of the participants was captured. There were documents provided by the participants. Some of the documents provided included: reports cards, progress reports, suspension letters, behavioral referrals, 504 Accommodation, IEP's, CSE determination letters, psychiatric evaluations, and behavior modification charts. Every document submitted was reviewed by this researcher and notes were taken on things of interest regarding the observations of those documents. Some of the parents had a methodical way of storing these documents in a binder or folders and were happy to bring them to the interview to share for this research study. Following the completion of the transcribed interviews, the researcher took the opportunity to listen to the recordings again and focus on taking notes to assist with the within-case analysis. The researcher was immersed in the data of each participant during the transcriptions and then listened to the recordings a second and sometimes a third time. The within-case analysis was performed one-by-one. When such analysis was concluded, the researcher moved to the next data set.

The descriptive phase of the data analysis was provided next. The immersion into the data was performed by listening to each case following the completion of transcription, reading through each transcription multiple times, and reviewing the documents provided by participants. During the course of reviewing the transcriptions this researcher highlighted significant words, phrases, and sentences. If the entire paragraph was of interest, it was highlighted as well. This comprehensive review of the data helped with the beginning stages of identifying patterns and themes. Notes taken during this process were added to the notebook containing the field notes.

Descriptive Phase

As the data analysis process began the descriptive phase was the initial area to be addressed. The descriptive phase consisted of the specific details surrounding the case itself, the setting involved, and the context. This process allowed for the study to be explained, the background of the research problem to be presented, and described the interviewing process. This phase produced the detail-rich descriptive data consistent with the case study methodology. The data reduction occurred during this phase to reduce data not pertinent to the overall research study. The result was thick and rich descriptions of this case. This chapter focused on the process used for data analysis.

Direct Interpretation

Following the descriptive phase, the direct interpretation of the data probed each instance of significant data to determine if there was meaning and/or significant occurrences contained therein. The cases were probed individually and held in light to the research question regarding parental treatment seeking experiences. During this phase, data was decomposed and then recomposed to deepen the understanding of the researcher and obtain meaning placed on each individual occurrence. The data was transcribed verbatim and this researcher conducted a line-by-line data analysis which consisted of highlighting meaningful texts and making notations in the margins while omitting text not relevant to the study. All data presented to the researcher was reviewed and data examined for any major rival explanations (Yin, 2009).

Categorical Aggregation

The data analysis continued with a categorical aggregation of the data. During this phase, the researcher was able to identify groups of data that were significant and meaningful among the multitude of data reviewed. The data identified was later placed in categorical groups for further review. Themes and patterns later evolved from such categorical groups. The researcher continued to move between the individual occurrences as presented by participants and the larger categories as they related to the research question. The categories were described by providing preliminary descriptive names and notations for each. The researcher used direct interpretation of the developing themes.

Within-Case Analysis

In a multiple-case study, it remains crucial the researcher examines individual cases for specific meanings and patterns. It is suggested at the beginning for the researcher to develop descriptions of the cases to organize and analyze the data in a comprehensive manner. One way Yin (2009) suggested assisting in the organization of the descriptive analysis was with the research questions. Despite using a multiple-case research design, each case must be examined individually for meanings and patterns. The individualized examination of each single-case comes at the beginning of the data analysis phase. The researcher attended to all the presenting evidence, considered all major rival interpretations, focused on significant aspects, and used prior knowledge within the analysis phase of this study (Yin, 2009).

All participants were interviewed separately, while the use of the same open-ended questions were utilized in semi-structured interviews. Member checking was incorporated in this study as this researcher emailed the data to the participants. The researcher encouraged participants to provide any additional data they felt would clarify this phenomenon and to correct any misunderstandings the researcher placed on the meaning of the data. Member checking is a process that upholds the validity in a research study. The researcher performed a within-case analysis initially on each single-case and made observations of the data provided, the patterns, and later themes as they evolved. One of the three main principles of data collection that assisted in establishing validity and reliability was using multiple sources of data; triangulation. The data consisted of verbatim interview transcripts, interview observations, researcher's field notes, and documents provided by participants.

This researcher reviewed the recordings within three days of the interview and took notes while listening to each. After each transcription, the recordings were reviewed a second time, where the transcripts were read for accuracy and additional notes taken. When moving through the transcripts the researcher highlighted relevant information that answered the research question and significant occurrences. The focus continued to remain on the single-case rather than making comparisons to other participant interviews. The identification and aggregation of themes were the main purpose of the within-case analysis while the researcher took copious notes of patterns in search of evolving themes. Finally, the researcher examined the categories to identify themes and patterns that occurred with participant quotes and longer passages and further clarified the present themes.

Cross-Case Analysis

The cross-case analysis began after the completion of the within-case analysis. The use of a multiple-case study design allowed the researchers to examine themes and patterns across cases using a similar design as a single-case study, while incorporating the same methodological framework (Yin, 2009). The researcher is expected to collect data through multiple methods which may include field notes, documentation, interviews, direct observations, archival records, participant observations, and physical artifacts (Yin, 2009). Yin (2009) reported researchers employed several key factors to ensure a high-quality analysis that includes: attending to all evidence, addressing possible rival interpretations, focusing on the more significant components, and integrating the use of prior subject matter expert knowledge within the case study. The process involved began with comparison between the first and second case. The continuation of this process examined each subsequent case while a comprehensive review of all transcripts, field notes, and replaying audio recordings, in search of patterns across data sets.

After the within-case analyses were concluded for all participants, this researcher obtained the confidential emails of each participant and forwarded a copy of their patterns for review of the accuracy of meanings placed on data. During the interview, session participants were advised they would be contacted by this researcher later, during the data analysis phase, to review and provide feedback on the patterns. Each participant was agreeable and offered a confidential email at that time whereby they could be contacted. Member checking plays a vital role as it allows for the verification of data. Member checking the information obtained and allowed for the data interpretation to be discussed and clarified with participants ensured accurate meaning(s).

All 10 participants provided feedback during the member checking process regarding the patterns they had received. Two of the participants made corrections for clarification, then the data was

resubmitted for later approval. After the member
checking phase, all 10 participants agreed with the
patterns presented to them. They offered any
additional help needed in the future and were eager to
hear overall findings and conclusions. Some of the
comments participants shared about the data:
"Amazing, you did a great job at hitting on all the
points! Dead on!" "Looks great to me." "Everything
looked perfect!" "Sounds about right." "Absolutely
perfect!" These comments served as confirmation the
interpretations were relevant to patterns the data were
a true and accurate representation of the participants'
experiences.

Immediately following each interview, field
notes were taken by the researcher to process
insights and perceptions about the participants'
experiences in seeking treatment for their children
diagnosed with ADHD. All participants said they had
documents they would like to share at the time of the
phone screening, however, three participants did not
provide documents to be reviewed. The seven
participants who did provide documents presented
them at the time of the interview or within a week
following the interview. All the participants were

encouraged to offer additional information they felt
would be helpful to this research study at the time the
member checking process was conducted. There was
clarification of the facts presented, but no additional
data provided at that time. One participant responded:

*I myself have never been diagnosed, but I feel
that I have always had ADD or some type of
ADHD. I didn't know if it would be important to
know that or state that in the paragraph, I don't
remember if I mentioned that during my
interview. The family history is correct and I do
still struggle on a daily basis to focus and pay
attention.*

The different sources of data; interview
observations, interviews, documents provided, all
served as a method of triangulation of data to
increase the research credibility.

Cross-Case Analysis

The cross-case analysis followed the
completion of the within-case analysis and it

attempted to broaden the statements of the observed occurrences. Every piece of data made available to the researcher was carefully examined, including each verbatim transcript, to search for common themes and patterns amongst the cases, as well as the complex meaning throughout the cases. At this stage, the researcher organized the presenting patterns into possible themes for determination later while examining the pertinent data available.

The patterns obtained from the within-case analysis from all 10 participants were entered into an Excel spreadsheet whereas the columns represented the patterns and quotes provided, the rows held the participant code numbers. This allowed the researcher to identify repeated patterns across cases. The researcher wrote down observed patterns across cases and observed they fell into three themes. Several actions for dependability were using triangulation of the verbatim transcripts, field notes, the documents provided by participants, and the researcher's personal journal. The researcher established dependability through several measures from procedures and methods to descriptive information that can reproduce by another researcher.

The researcher incorporated rich and thick descriptions of the research that allowed the readers to step into the experiences of the participants (Creswell, 2013). Including these aspects and others increased the acceptability as a trustworthy research design and the research findings.

Overview of Themes and Patterns

The experiences of the parent participants were expressed in response to the open-ended questions and the subsequent data was obtained from those responses. The objective of the interview was to answer the research question "What is the experience of parents in seeking treatment for their child who is diagnosed with ADHD?" A listing of the patterns and themes were procured from the verbatim transcripts, field notes, documents provided, and member checking. It was evident there were considerable challenges present in the experiences of parents who have sought treatment for their child's ADHD diagnosis. The next section will provide a description of each of the listed themes and their patterns will be further expressed. The participants'

words were directly quoted to illustrate the patterns
and themes.

Presentation of the Data and Results of the Analysis

The researcher analyzed available data, in this
case study and identified significant occurrences that
would bring a deeper understanding of the research
inquiry that came in part from participant comments. It
is essential for any researcher to conduct due
diligence in assessing for alternative explanations of
occurrences (Rowley, 2002). The study included
direct quotations from each of the 10 participants who
assisted in formulating the patterns and themes that
evolved. The use of direct quotations woven
throughout will allow the researcher and readers to
understand the experiences in a detailed, informative
manner (Creswell, 2007).

The participants all agreed to meet with this
researcher at a scheduled time at a professional
office to participate in the research interview. All
participants arrived within 10 minutes of the
scheduled time. Some did arrive visibly anxious about
the proceedings, but later observed to be comfortable

within the setting. The process was explained to each participant before starting the interview and an opportunity to ask questions was extended at that time. None of the participants had any questions; this signified they understood what was explained to them. The professional office had a desk and chairs, bookshelves, and a large window that offered plenty of natural light. Most the interviews were held during daylight hours; some were held during the early evening. All the participants were given the opportunity to suggest the day and time that worked best for them; every attempt was made to oblige, including an 8:00 a.m. session.

The participants shared their experiences of seeking treatment for their children diagnosed with ADHD. The participants were open and made attempts to express their experiences in a way that others could understand their journey. Participants generally used multiple words and examples to ensure the researcher understood the nuances, programs, and treatment types to which they were referring. Participants wanted to convey – despite the challenges that had arisen in seeking treatment – their desire to help their child and see them succeed was the driving force behind continued advocacy and relentless search for the right treatment. Several parents cried during points of the interview as they described how the symptoms and often comorbidity affected their child's overall functioning. Despite the parents' best efforts to obtain the proper treatment, they were met with road blocks, inconsistency, and a lack of direction and resources. The pain that emanated from one of the mothers as she described her daughter without a best friend, eating lunch without engaging with others, and being socially inept. One could sense how deeply this had affected this parent. The child had counseling services in school, yet the services were not being provided to her. A second mother shared her story; she begged for someone to tell her, "How can I help my daughter." What should she do, what treatment will fix her problems? As tears streamed down her face she concluded that specific direction was what she needed. A third mother (licensed nurse) spoke about lack of direction and resources and her husband telling her she "should be able to fix her son, because she is a nurse." With tears filling her eyes she described telling him fixing this condition was not her

area of expertise and above her pay grade. The
overall running theme throughout that emerged was
the lack of available support for parents and children
diagnosed with ADHD.

Nine of the 10 parents were employed, with the
last one being unemployed and on disability. Some of
the parents worked with children in the capacity of a
social worker, school nurse, teaching assistant in a
special education classroom, and school bus aide for
children who are classified in the special education
program. Those parents were aware of the symptoms
of ADHD and allowed that knowledge to drive their
relentless efforts to find the treatment best suited to
their children's needs. In all 10 cases, the parents
described multiple methods and modalities they
sought to help mediate the ADHD symptoms. Even
parents who found medication management to be
beneficial for their children described multiple
medications tried and various titration of medication
episodes. The search for treatment can be viewed as
an ongoing effort that required a significant amount of
parental stamina. Some parents offered their
preference modality in treating ADHD, but reported
they were open and willing to try whatever they were

told would work. In a few of the cases, the parents appeared to be waiting for the researcher to offer them specific solutions for their child's ADHD symptoms.

There were three themes that emerged from the data analysis. The first theme was the treatment seeking experience was filled with many challenges and difficulties resulted in a negative treatment seeking experience. The next theme was compounding challenges parents faced when interfacing with the school system. The third theme was the lack of support parents felt they received or were offered.

Theme One: Persistent School System Challenges

In nine of the 10 cases, participants shared their difficulties in working with their children's school systems in seeking treatment and collaborating with them on behalf of their children diagnosed with ADHD. This was a surprising theme to evolve, as this researcher presumed the greatest difficulties would be expressed through outside medical facilities and had disclosed such in the ethical biases section of this dissertation. Talking about the school experience brought out intense participants' responses that provoked many to tears and others to anger. The parents shared perspectives of how they felt the school system failed to meet their child's needs, lack of staff knowledge and experience, withholding of mandated services, or in some cases exacerbated presenting symptoms. Parents described examples of events that stayed with them two, four, and in one case, seven years. Within the school system, there is a federal program (504 Accommodation) for students meeting eligibility criteria. A 504 is via the Americans with Disabilities Act and attempts to level the field for students with disabilities by providing students with learning needs' services and accommodations toward educational success.

Pattern 1 (a): 504 Accommodation not being Implemented or Offered

The first pattern was children having a 504 Accommodation not being implemented. ADHD is a diagnosis recognized as a handicapping condition that allows individuals to be considered for a 504

Accommodation. In every parent's case with a 504 Accommodation in place, the parents described examples of the 504 Accommodation not being utilized to the child's detriment. One mother spoke about how she had to teach her children what 504 Accommodation to which each of them were entitled, because the school system routinely denied and or overlooked the listed items. One mother discussed how she prepared her children to respond in cases when their 504's were not being implemented.

> *I educated my children, because I'm not there all the time, so if you know that they're not giving you what you're supposed to, then you've got to stand up and you're allowed to stand up for yourself and say 'no this is wrong.'*

This mother responded to a teacher informing her daughter who had asked the teacher if the she knew the daughter had a 504. The mother said her children were anxious each year because of non-implementation experience of the 504 Accommodation. "Not all the teachers follow them. They break the rules." Another mom described having

to contact three staff members who were supposed to
be providing services and 504 Accommodation, all of
whom denied knowing about a 504. When another
mom asked if the school thought her son (struggling
academically) could use a 504, they quickly said a
504 wasn't needed. "We had asked about a 504, and
we were told because it did not appear to be
impacting his education at that point, we didn't need
to go that route."

*Nothing was offered to me, a 504, anything. I
didn't even know those things existed.
(Participant One)*

*And I said and if they still don't give it to you
that's when you remove yourself because you
have your pass and you go to your guidance
counselor. And then you tell your guidance
counselor I'm trying to advocate for myself, it's
not working. This teacher is not giving me what
I need or they're arguing with me whatever it
may be and that has helped as well because
now that sheds light on what's going on in the
classrooms. (Participant Two)*

*He's had a 504 when he was first diagnosed
and then, I wish I never did it but we dropped
that in middle school. He was on medication
and he was doing well and his guidance
counselor suggested that he didn't need that
anymore because he was doing fine
considering his grades from elementary school.
So I dropped the 504 and it was like a huge
mistake. It was a huge mistake, I regret it. So,
once he got back into high school we're like we
need to go back to this again because it was
like the most horrible thing that he didn't have
that in middle school, because I went along
with what a guidance counselor suggested.
There were times though where I was feeling
frustrated because I wasn't sure if the teachers
were really following the 504. Even in high
school too I wasn't sure that they were doing
everything they could. (Participant Three)*

*I mostly go to the teachers first. And none of
them were saying let's go with a 504. I didn't
realize that you could go for ADHD. I thought it*

was mostly for learning disabilities so but I
guess the teachers aren't allowed to say
anything because they don't want to spend any
more money out of pocket if they don't have to.
(Participant Four)

Then they told me at the end of last meeting oh
he doesn't have a 504 plan. I'm like yes he
does. I gave you the prescription and you put it
in place. So, she's like if you want that for next
year then we have to have another meeting.
Yeah, I want that. Let's start that. I still haven't
heard nothing from them. What I heard from
them was did you get that one letter?
(Participant Five)

He gets extra time to do tests. They're
supposed to take him out of the class so that
he has a quieter place to do and he can
concentrate better. That didn't happen. And I
just, every year I go back and every year I'm
like why isn't this happening. Well because it's
quiet in the class. That's what I get told. Well
ok but he's still around all of his friends. He

needs the extra time. I'm not asking you to take
him out of his class, I'm asking for him to be
taken out of his class to do the tests so. Like I
had said. I'm hoping this year because he's
going into middle school things will be different.
But I don't know. I don't know when it comes to
the 504 plan. I don't know, how far to push it.
So, but that's mostly the discouraged issue for
me. I mean they're very ... his school system
he goes to they were more than happy to help
me but it almost seemed to me that they didn't
want to follow through with it, so. (Author's
Note: "...the school system noted appeared to
be happy to help the parent, but when the help
was needed they did not follow through.")
(Participant Six)

Sometimes I was feeling like some teachers
just weren't doing everything that they could for
him. So, I'm like I have this 504 in place and
there's times it just didn't feel like he was
getting the help that he needed. So, it was a bit
frustrating with the school. (Participant Eight)

So, they got all the way until November and
never noticed he had a 504 in place. So, my
husband is like how do you guys not realize
that he has a 504? Like how do we get from
September to November and we had gotten
numerous calls home for behavior. (Participant
Nine)

Pattern 1 (b): School Staff Lacked Training, Knowledge, and Effective Response to Students with ADHD

Several parents spoke about how school staff responded to their children with ADHD and how their lack of knowledge about the diagnosis sometimes exacerbated the negative behaviors the children expressed. One mother described through tears how the principal of her child's elementary school directed her to keep her son at home for two weeks. The mother felt this was highly inappropriate, but she did not know how to fight against it. She said the principal would call.

It was just "your kid's out of control come pick him up" every day. To the point at one time she told me to keep him home for two weeks. So, then the next year, I put my foot down. And the first day of school I was in the principal's office saying this can't happen again and she recommended the 504 plan and that was put in place [pretty] quickly.

She described there being a new principal the following year to whom she spoke about her son's condition. She later described that despite her obtaining a 504 quickly, having it implemented was another struggle. Other parents described not feeling heard by the school system or feeling staff did not care for various reasons.

My greatest challenges would be the fact that everybody seems to think or from the feeling I get is that this has never happened before. And he has ADHD, it's a pretty common thing. So, I mean, we should have plans in place for children like that. (Participant One)

A teacher is not going to see that. A teacher is not going to understand that. And this is where not understanding ADHD and anxiety and all that together, now she's looked at as a child who is not listening, a child who's being disrespectful. (Participant Two)

The teacher said, she's like well I'm not going to tell you what to do because, I guess they're brainwashed not to say anything because they think there's a problem. They're with my child seven hours a day. (Participant Four)

*The barrier is the school. They don't ...
(Author's Note: "...the school system didn't advocate for the participant's child as she would have expected...") they're not advocates for the kids. It's like they don't really care. They just want to push them along or keep them back. Or, set up new programs for the kids that can't get through and call it different names. Just call it what it is. You failed my kid. It's like they just don't care. They just dropped the ball. They don't care, just my*

take on things, they just don't care. Because if
they cared they would do what they had to do
to get him what he needed. Or tell me maybe,
do you need anything? But no they don't care.
(Participant Five)

So, but that's mostly the discouraging issue
for me. I mean they're very, his school system
that he goes to they were more than happy to
help me but it almost seemed to me that they
didn't want to follow through with it.
(Participant Six)

Well he needs to go to the hospital. When I
spoke with the pediatrician, the psychiatrist,
and the counselor, they said 'absolutely not,'
... for what he was exhibiting the hospital
wouldn't have even admitted him. (Participant
Seven)

None of his teachers were very good at all as
far as reaching out to him. They just they're
like this is a child who doesn't want to do his
work. He doesn't want to participate, they just

*brushed him aside. The journey itself has
been quite a struggle. The medication that's
been fine but school has been the toughest
part through this whole thing. (Participant
Eight)*

*We got that from one of our, from one of the
teachers. Well you do know your son is
special ed. Okay? Well special ed kids are not
always as successful as mainstream students.
But they don't want them to be successful
because they're those kids. I told you, well the
whole you know your son is special ed? I was
like what does that mean? Oh I don't mean it
the way I said it. Oh, yeah you did. And that's
exactly what I said, oh yeah you did. Oh, no I
think you misunderstood me. No I didn't
misunderstand you at all. And my husband he
puts his arm on mine. And I'm like what, we're
just going to leave that right now and let's
focus on what we were discussing because I
could see the mom in me become very
unprofessional in a mom way. (Participant
Nine)*

I don't think schools are equipped to handle
the amount of children that have [those]
needs. And I think a lot of them get lost in the
mix. (Participant Ten)

Pattern 1 (c): School Staff Provided Limited
Information, Resources, and Guidance for
Parents.

Parents described the difficulty in wanting to
help their children, but being unable because they
themselves did not know what they could do to
remedy the behaviors reported by the school. The
parents relied on the school to provide direction to
them assuming the schools were the experts in
working with children. That help did not come. One
parent spoke about how she could not understand if
all these professionals were trained in early childhood
in her son's class, then why did they not see what was
wrong with her son? They never mentioned ADHD to
her nor suggested resources to improve her son's
behaviors.

*The 1st day of school he got into a fist fight, so
that was basically it. A lot of his behavioral
problems, the school calling me almost every
day about it. He did this today. He did that
today. And then it was basically taken upon me
to take him to his pediatrician and say listen
this is what we're going through every single
day. We need to figure something out.
(Participant One)*

*Like kind of help me a little bit like tell me like
what can I do but it's not just in those certain
crisis it's with a child who does have these
different things. Maybe having the resources,
like having a list of the resources like here's all
the autistic resources that I know. Here's all the
ADHD resources that I know about. This is a
support group for parents. These are a couple
of therapists that do different types of therapy.
Like literally something like that. Like a sheet of
paper, you could hand me that I could just be
like know reputable people that they've done
their research on that they know. Like
something that I think would be helpful for a*

parent with a child like that with ADHD or autism. I'm just saying that's something that could benefit a parent who might not know where to go and maybe because there is that back and forth between them, the student and the parent that could be something that might be helpful. (Participant Two)

So, once we get to 6th grade they started the testing program. It's like they wanted me to take him to the doctors. Take him to the pediatrician, have them first look at him and then we'll start da, da, this and that. And I'm like really? Why do I have to do all the work? Isn't that your job? (Participant Five)

The only system that I ever had to feel like, go against was the school. That's the only one and that goes right along with trying to figure out what's best for him. That's the only system I had to go for. (Participant Six)

I could have taken him to three different doctors and if I needed to have but nobody,

they were too busy telling me that oh you have
to pick him up. He's suspended out of school.
He's got in school suspension. He's in
kindergarten. How does he get suspended out
of school? (Participant Seven)

The school doesn't provide resources. Not for
the parent anyhow, they don't. There's no
seminars that say, if your child has (ADHD).
So, the school itself, no, no, and special ed and
especially kids with ADHD behavior is not on
their priority list. It's not, unfortunately, it's not.
(Participant Nine)

Pattern 1 (d): The Role of Advocacy in ADHD and School

Advocating on behalf of the needs and rights of one's child diagnosed with ADHD was prevalent among many of the 10 participants. They spoke about the role of advocacy when interfacing with school personnel, during 504 Accommodation and special education meetings, and when their children's accommodations were not being fully implemented.

One mother spoke about how she often went to meetings prepared to fight for her daughter because the school would often attempt to remove the very accommodations that were helping her daughter to be successful. Other parents echoed the same sentiment during meetings where they were met with staff that did not feel their child needed special accommodations.

And every day it's a struggle and I'm constantly having to fight for him. Fighting the school for the things he should get. (Participant One)

So, I feel a lot of self-advocating unfortunately the parents have to do so much on their own. There's not a lot out there to guide you and to kind of fight with you, you got to do a lot of it on your own... it takes a certain kind of parent to do that because not all parents have that push in them, or they have more fear, or they hear oh you're not allowed to get that, or you're not allowed to do that. They don't know their rights. Very important to know your rights. Huge thing to know your rights. (Participant Two)

*I always tell him, you have to advocate for
yourself, especially in the high school. They
don't want to see parents advocating for their
kids there. (Participant Four)*

*You got to be your own advocate and there's
parents out there that can't be their advocates
because they're too busy working trying to
provide for their family. And if you're not your
own advocate you got to go get an advocate.
No, you got to go do everything on your own.
And if you're not your own advocate you got to
go get an advocate. Even though the lady was
an advocate at the special services she barely
called me. She called me once maybe two
times just to tell me when the appointment
was. She's supposed to be my advocate?
You're supposed to be speaking for me and my
child. Basically you work for the freaking school
system so you ain't advocate nothing. You
probably have too many, so many kids out
there that need the help that you're
overwhelmed that you don't have enough*

people to help you. (Participant Five)

*I think if you're an educated parent and I don't
mean educated as in smart, I think if you have
the resources to get you the information that
makes you an educated parent. I think an
educated parent who has a voice for their child
will be very successful. I think if you're an
uneducated parent, you don't know the system,
you don't know what you're qualified for, you
don't you know, know any of that or throw in a
language barrier ... (Participant Nine)*

*As far as the services from school I always
went to those meetings prepared to fight for
what I needed for her but they were
accommodating in giving us what we needed.
(Participant Ten)*

Theme Two: Difficult Treatment Seeking Experience

Nine of the 10 participants spoke about the
difficulties they had in seeking treatment for their

child's diagnosis of ADHD. Those difficulties were found in the school system, in the community, and in the offices of medical and professional providers. Several participants spoke about the misdiagnosis their children received and in those cases, ADHD was not included in the discussion of possible explanations of the child's behavior. One mother spoke about how she feels she was not given the diagnosis of ADHD early enough, that it directly affected her son later becoming diagnosed with ODD. She also outlined several professionals working with her son in school and beyond who had not spoken about ADHD. "We even went to a counselor that advertised they are one of the leading ADHD counselors (their forte) and never once did he utter the words to me 'he's got ADHD'." This same mom reports her son was prescribed Focalin following her presented concerns to her doctor, however at that time, there was no medical discussion that her son had ADHD. She later found out Focalin was a drug commonly used for treating ADHD. Another participant described going to her pediatrician:

And the pediatrician didn't think he had definite signs of ADHD. At first he was diagnosed with possible Asperger's, then Sensory Integration Disorder, and then it was moved onto they weren't sure because they thought it was just behavioral. And then finally they decided after they did a Conner's and a couple other tests, getting his teachers involved, that he did have ADHD.

Stigma came up as a factor that made the treatment seeking experience difficult. Parents experienced both internal and external forces of stigma. This largely influenced their beliefs about treatment and impacted their own emotional health and social influences. Some parents blamed themselves for their children having ADHD or not being able to 'fix them.' There was self-doubt and feelings of not being heard.

Pattern Two (a) The Effects of Stigma on the Treatment Seeking Experience

It would be difficult to overlook the effects of stigma on the treatment seeking experience. There are many negative effects of stigma for parents seeking treatment for their children which encompasses over-medicating children for behavioral disorders, the long-term developmental effects on children accepting medications, and stigmatizing beliefs (dos Reis et al., 2010). Stigma can come from one's social group, community, cultural influences, or within themselves. When one acts contrary to those beliefs, it can raise self-doubt and blame. Stigma can also influence a parents' perception they are not being heard by family or practitioners.

This person's not really listening to me. You can tell they're not listening to me. And then emotionally you sort of feel trapped because you're the person responsible for this child's well-being. And what ends up happening is you internalize it and it becomes, 'it's my fault.' I am

*missing something. I am doing something
wrong. And I am missing that one piece that
could help her and I don't know what it is. And I
feel like because I'm her mom it's my
responsibility. So therefore I take the brunt of it.
I take that pain that I'm feeling for her and I
don't know what to do with it. (Participant Two)*

*Personally, I found it really difficult to put my
child on medication that he was going to be
taking for years to come. That was the hardest
part for me. I tried to do like herbal like things
that might help him focus. I tried things like that
for the longest time. And it just was never
enough and I really did not want to put him on
medication. I had a really hard time with that. I
was like I did not want to put my child on
medication but once I spoke to his teacher and
she said how much harder the next grade level
was going to be for him if he was not on
medication I just broke down and did it.
(Participant Three)*

Now I don't know if he really is ADD because you know some doctors, it's just an easy diagnosis, I feel. Yeah your kid got ADD. Let's just give him a medicine and he'll be fine. And like I started crying in the office because I'm like I don't want my kid to be classified with ADD or take, not even that, just to take the medicine. I don't want my kid on medication. So, I refuse to give it to him in the summer. He don't need it. What does he need to focus on – games? (Participant Five)

Psychologically it has been hard because even where I have stumbled it was my fault. It was my parenting that created this monster. That's all I've been told. (Participant Seven)

For us it was frustrating in the beginning because I felt like I was pretty educated, I work in the field. How do I not know how to fix my child, what was wrong with him, did I do something? You know how could I make it better? And my husband was like you should be able to fix him because you know this is

your field. And I'm like this is not my realm.
This is way above even me as a mom, let
alone a professional ... you are kind of
helpless. (Participant Nine)

But her father had a totally different view. You
know she's just a kid, this is just a phase, she'll
just grow out of it. And I think we both agreed
that medication is not something that we
wanted for her but I think it hurt his pride to
know that she was different, and she needed
counseling, and that she was always going to
be different than the rest of the kids. And that
hurt him. And I could understand that. It was
hard reacting to that and knowing what her
deficiencies were but that's what you do as a
parent. You support the child and you move on
and deal with that. (Participant Ten)

Pattern Two (b) What it is like Navigating Systems for ADHD Treatment

Many of the participants had strong reactions
to this sub-research question, yet the common thread

among them was the difficulty they faced in their
pursuits. There were several areas through the
interviews where participants reached back in time
and you could sense their deep pain for what they
had experienced. This was one of those questions
that seemed to do just that. Some apologized for
becoming emotional and were assured there was no
need for apologies, to take their time and share what
they would like. Parents described what their
experiences navigating systems for ADHD treatment
was like.

> *Um it's like it's the 1st time it's ever being
> done. Nobody ever knows what the next step
> is. Or everybody's got different
> recommendations so you are kind of just
> drowning and trying to figure it out, what you're
> going do next. For me it's just nobody has ever
> been like okay this is what you need to do next.
> Just a lot of recommendations, especially for
> me doing it alone, it's stressful. Um the
> pediatrician said take him to see a therapist,
> then a psychiatrist and that's one thing that's
> all in its own trying to figure out the difference*

between a therapist, a psychiatrist, a
counselor. (Participant One)

Mostly unfortunately mostly it's internet related.
Just doing a lot of research on the internet. I
haven't really found out, I'm surprised that I
haven't found people in person talking about it
and saying hey I heard there's a group or
there's not a lot of talk about it. What about
ADHD? What about that? Where is the support
groups for that like why is it not as, there's not
much out there? Or at least maybe it's out
there and it's just not as, not as known and
maybe I'm maybe I'm missing it maybe, I don't
know. I feel just like, just like I'm navigating on
my own on the internet, finding little bits and
pieces of things and trying to put it all together
but um I'm not finding it very helpful at all
getting help for issues with ADHD for myself or
for my child. (Participant Two)

There were times though where I was feeling
frustrated because I wasn't sure if the teachers
were really following the 504. Even in high

school too I wasn't sure that they were doing everything they could. Sometimes I was feeling like some teachers just weren't doing everything that they could for him. So, I'm like I have this 504 in place, and there's times it just didn't feel like he was getting the help that he needed. So, it was a bit frustrating with the school. (Participant Three)

Hard, it's very difficult. I was like put to this person then put to this person. And it' kind of hard to navigate really if you don't know a lot of people. When you know a lot of people it seems like it's very easy. Like I didn't know he could get a 504. I thought they had to diagnose him with a learning disability to get a 504. So, if you don't know somebody who knows the ins and outs then it's hard. I didn't know there was a parent advocate like you could just talk to like anytime. (Participant Four)

It sucks. It stinks. It's frustrating. They don't make it easy for you. They don't make it simple for you. They don't make the process, okay

you got to do this, do this, do this. Basically
you're just thrown out to the wolves. Basically
you're on your own. (Participant Five)

Oh, dear Lord. Climbing up Mount Everest.
Swimming in the ocean without even a noodle.
(Participant Seven)

I think if you don't have the resources it's
definitely a nightmare to get through. I think
finding the right information is very difficult. So,
I think unless you know somebody whose child
is successful with that diagnosis you almost
want to go to them and be like okay like why
are you so successful with this diagnosis?
What did you do to get your child to this point
that's what I want. I want my child to be
successful. How do I get there? But a lot of
times you see the other parents sinking in the
water with you. So, you know again you're
talking this didn't work for that person so I
didn't want to try or this one didn't, and this one
and this one, you try to hang onto the what
worked for people and try to piece it together

but I think if you don't have that one person
who is successful kind of thing it's hard. You
know I think again there's not that support
there so it's very hard to navigate the system in
itself or get the support that you need.
(Participant Nine)

It's challenging because like I said because it's
such a common diagnosis now that you don't
know as a parent what treatments your child
needs, what they should be doing different.
(Participant Ten)

Pattern Two (c): Multiple methods of treatment used to mediate the ADHD symptoms

This pattern was present across all 10 cases where parents sought multiple methods of treatment to address their children's ADHD symptoms. Parents reported using herbal remedies, change of diet, diet restrictions, removal of red dye #40, behavior modifications, counseling, psychiatry, and medications. For those who used medications, they used multiple medications before finding the one that worked or titrated up or down on medications before settling with the right dosage. Some parents spoke about feeling judged because they sought medication but wanted the provider to know they had tried everything else and it had not worked. One mom stated, "That first medication did not work at all. Second medication did not work at all. Third medication is very good and there is a huge difference with my son ..." Another mom described her son who was in 4th grade being on six different medications and the one he was currently taking was no longer working. She said he was doing well on Concerta for about a month and states she plans on returning to the pediatrician because it is no longer effective.

> *And he still struggled in school on the*
> *medication, I had even tried a different*
> *medication after that summer when he had a*
> *break, he went back on the medication he was*
> *on and he had side effects and we then tried a*
> *different one from there and that one still*
> *wasn't any better so we just went off*
> *medication all together. (Participant Three)*

He started off with the lowest dose of
Concerta; it's the extended release at 18 mg.
And, he then went up to 27 and there were,
extended periods of time in between each of
these increases. Then he went to the 36. When
the 36 was no longer seeming to be effective.
He was going through a growth spurt. His body
chemistry seemed to be going haywire; the
pediatrician wanted to go up to 54. And, that
seemed to me to be a big number at the time,
so we negotiated to do a half [increase].
(Participant Eight)

My husband and I went a homeopathic route to
begin with. We changed his diet and increased
exercise. And, did everything we could possibly
research and find information on and it was not
working. We wound up going with a natural
supplement, we'll say. At that time a
homeopathic remedy seemed to work for a
little while. (Participant Nine)

Theme Three: Lack of support

The lack of support that parents felt was significant and encompassed several areas of life from social and familial supports to community supports and available resources. Some participants spoke about the marital strain evident prior to and during the treatment seeking experience. Spouses were sometimes at odds over the origin of the ADHD behaviors and later had difficulty agreeing what would be the best remedy for such behavior. One mother said her husband was influenced by stigma and reluctant to treat their son's ADHD.

So, he was not on board at all. And it came to a point in our marriage where we were headed in very different directions. And we sat down and I said either we come up with a better game plan or we have to go our separate ways, because it was creating a horrible, horrible tension in our marriage and in our household. And my son's behavior was getting worse. It wasn't getting any better.

Another mom described the difficulty her son had in doing his homework due to the ADHD diagnosis and her husband was not as supportive as she had hoped he would be. She described how he responded and she reacted, "Oh just leave him alone. No. Shut up! You didn't pass school. You want your kid to be like a nobody? I want my kid to go to college." Another mother described her spouse's response, "Her father and I didn't always agree on the diagnosis or the treatment. He was the type of person that would say it's 'something she'll grow out of'." At the time of the interview the two were separated. The lack of available resources for ADHD and help within the participants' communities echoed throughout the cases. Moms referred to the abundance of available programs and groups for Autism, but the lack of such for ADHD.

Pattern Three (a): Lack of Community Support and Resources

The lack of community support and resources for children with ADHD was a common plight among participants. They spoke about their desire to have information and someone leading them towards the best treatment, the best responses, and the best way to help their children, but found none. Some moms described using their connections to Autism groups as a support for their child's ADHD when they realized the gap in ADHD support groups.

With tears streaming down her face one mother begged to be given the resources she needs to help her child.

> *The difference is, like I said, there's not as much information and not enough support groups and help to kind of help me along and I feel like I'm doing it a little bit more as opposed to on my own when I was fighting for the autism part of it.*

> *There seems to be a very big focus on helping children with Autism which is wonderful for us because I have two autistic children. But, the ADHD part of that um I'm not finding even with the psychiatrist, I'm not finding any information as to where to go to help the child with that*

part. Tell me what to do as a parent to help
with that part of it. (Participant Two)

I wish that earlier on that there were other
avenues for support. The support group that
we do go to is a help, but that seems to be just
about it. (Participant Seven)

I definitely don't think there's enough psych
help out there for both parents and the child
involved. I think sometimes these kids are too
immature to process all the emotions they're
going through. But, there really isn't anywhere
for a) the parent to go; or b) for the student to
go or the kid to go to talk to somebody about
those kind of things. (Participant Nine)

When she was younger, I found a support
group of parents with children with special
needs. It was just a group of parents, local
parents, and the first time I went I noticed it
was four parents and we all graduated from
high school together the same year. Two of the
parents, the children were autistic, the one was

nonverbal, the other was nonverbal but
learning to speak, and the third was Pervasive
Developmental Disorder, not otherwise
specified. And, then there's my child who didn't
quite fit in and didn't have a diagnosis at that
time. Nothing through the community, nothing
through the schools, and it could be I didn't
reach out for it or I didn't know anything was
available. (Participant Ten)

Pattern Three (b): Lack of Social and Familial Supports

The lack of social and familial supports the
parents found appeared to cause isolation and
increase the stress and frustration they felt in the
overall treatment seeking process. There were stories
of family members who offered advice, but they were
not parenting a child with ADHD, which caused
contention among the parents receiving that advice.
Others spoke about how the lack of social supports
affected them socially and emotionally.

Social - I missed a lot of things socially that we can't do because for two years he can't eat specific foods; we couldn't do things like that. Socially - like today he missed half of, a good chunk of his basketball practice, because he could not focus on the coach. And, he could not stand still. He was all over the place, so socially it's been stressful that way. Emotionally on me. I've cried way more times than I could count, because it's just frustrating and there's nothing you could do really - it's been hard.

Others spoke about missing outings with friends, being able to obtain a childcare provider for them to go out socially, and limited social involvement for their children outside of organized sports and activities.

I have my boyfriend and my mom, but a lot of times I feel like with my mom, it's not her responsibility to deal with it, and I could call her to complain but that's all I could do. My boyfriend's there, so he financially supports us,

but he's not the one making the medical
decisions and stuff like that. So, a lot of the
medical stuff especially with him falls on me.
And it's stressful. (Participant One)

Um I want to say that I'm sure he (referring to
her husband) doesn't think that he has it. We're
not on good terms right now so it's hard for me
to um. We're going through marriage
counseling right now so. Things are a little up
in the air right now. (Participant Five)

My sister sometimes thinks, even now, that he
doesn't need it (referring to medication). And I
kind of look at my sister, and you have a two
and a four-year old. And it's not that her
opinion doesn't matter, but you have a two-
and a four-year old. You have a husband. I've
done this with him by myself for eleven years.
(Participant Six)

I'm going to say the social impact; my social
circle dwindled to about nothing. Because, I
could not accept invitations that people that

most average people, they want to do

something, they go get a babysitter. You do

what you go to do and I could not just get any

babysitter. My family, I could not use for just

any social outing, because it was hard for them

too. So yeah, my social life was severely

impacted. I'm not going to say completely,

weed out ... the good ones will stick through.

But, psychologically, it was lonely to not have

support. (Participant Seven)

Thematic Synthesis

The data in this study was analyzed using
Robert Yin's (2009) model for case study analysis.
The information contained in this study was
decomposed into smaller parts by the researcher then
later recomposed with significant meaning. The use of
prior knowledge as suggested by Yin (2009) was
used during this process to minimize errors. The data
was maintained in a systematic way from
organization, categorization, and later analysis of
single occurrences later clustered into patterns.
Themes were then formed from the overall main

components of the research phenomenon. The researcher followed Yin's (2009) recommendation of focusing on the most significant components of the case.

Three themes emerged from the data. Theme one was school system challenges. Most mothers reported significant difficulties interfacing with the school system. One of the most prevalent challenges was 504 Accommodation not being offered and in other cases having a 504 Accommodation not being implemented. Parents watched as their children struggled academically yet they had a method on paper that should have helped their child, but instead it did not go beyond the paper on which it was written. Some participants expressed anger and frustration that they had to continually monitor if their child was receiving the services for which they were eligible and having to inform school staff the 504 existed. Parents spoke about school staff that lacked proper training and knowledge about the ADHD disorder and therefore often responded ineffectively to the needs of children. One mom cried as she said her daughter was labeled the bad one or disrespectful because she called out often in class. Meanwhile, many children with ADHD have difficulty with calling out and interrupting conversations. Parents had expected a school system that specializes in working with children would be able to provide them with information and resources on one of the most common childhood disorders in America. Parents overwhelmingly experienced a lack of direction and guidance from schools. There was little-to-no information provided to parents, recommendations for helping their child with the presenting symptoms, or referrals to community programs, groups, or other were provided. One mom spoke through tears as she explained how she felt working with the school system trying to figure out how to help her daughter. She repeated that she wanted someone to tell her something she could do as a mom to help her. That guidance, information, and resources never came. Advocating within the school system appeared to stir many internal emotions within participants. They spoke about being ready to fight, and the importance of advocating for their children with ADHD. The advocacy was demonstrated with 504 Accommodation, pursuing special bussing, and obtaining other services their children needed. The only parent who did not experience a negative school encounter concerning her son's ADHD diagnosis was a mother who is a clinical social worker, who specializes in working with children with mental illness and behavior disorders. Nine other parents experienced meaningful adverse responses in their school experience.

The second theme that emerged was the difficulty parents had in their treatment seeking experience. Most parents reported negative encounters when they were asked about their treatment seeking experience and specifically their experience navigating systems for ADHD treatment. Some of the words used to describe it were "torture, swimming in the ocean without a noodle" and other metaphors demonstrating the extreme difficulties they faced. One of the areas that made for a negative experience was the stigma associated with the ADHD diagnosis and ADHD treatment. Parents encountered stigma externally and internally. Those incidents of stigma sparked self-doubt, questioning, and affected the treatment parents were willing to engage. Every parent described using multiple methods of treatment or in cases where medication was the preferred treatment, there were multiple types of medication used, or varied titrations of medications before finishing the right dosage. Sometimes after finding the right dose parents had to return to the doctor because the medication stopped being effective.

The third theme was the lack of support experienced by parents. The lack of support caused parents to feel isolated and impacted their emotional and psychological well-being. Parents felt family and friends did not understand what it was like parenting a child with ADHD. One mother remarked about her anger when others would say they also had a child with ADHD, when she knew they did not have the disorder. She furthered it by explaining she felt like people were dismissing the daily struggle she went through as they joined in with 'me, too.' Some parents described their families remarking their children just needed a spanking or corporal punishment to straightened them out. This often came from the grandparents of the children and in all cases the mothers described this with difficulty demonstrating the great divide of understanding of the etiology of ADHD. Parents consistently spoke about the lack of support and included the lack of community support and resources. Parents were unable to find any support groups, programs, training, or other resources to help them parent their children with ADHD. Some parents likened ADHD to Autism and asked, 'where is our help?', given there is so much available for the Autism community? To mediate this issue, some parents relied on the support of the Autism community, although it did not provide specific resources they needed for their child's AHDD diagnosis.

Eight of the 10 mothers concluded the interview appearing worn from the stories they told. Some shed tears during the interview, while others raised their voices in anger for their experience. There was joy at the triumphs like conquering the school meeting by showing up with an advocate and adding special bussing on a 504 Accommodation. With all the sharing, there was a sense the struggle is ever present, the battle not yet won, but each parent was committed to seeing their children through.

Interpretative Phase

The interpretative phase is the final stage in the data analysis process where the researcher developed generalizations obtained from the data used in this study and then used the interpreted data to inform the research community of lessons learned. This allowed the researcher to analyze the research findings, present what the data uncovered, and identify how the findings may be relevant to parents seeking treatment for their children diagnosed with ADHD. Chapter 5 will include a more detailed description of the occurrences in this phase.

Some trends were increasingly clear as the data was analyzed, as they related to the difficult experience the majority of parents encountered in their pursuit of treatment for their child's ADHD diagnosis. Nine of the mothers reported difficulty working with their children's school systems, stigma and blame, limited familial and social supports, and scarce community resources. Advocating for the needs of their children became paramount when attending school meetings, and being connected to an advocate from within the school was not always helpful. Parents remarked about feeling like they were a burden and that teachers may not have been permitted to advocate for children because of the cost the district may incur.

Parents spoke about noticing the symptoms of ADHD very early, even if not associated with the ADHD diagnosis. Several parents thought it was the terrible twos and their children would grow out of that stage. For those that did not report seeing behaviors as early as two years old, they reported seeing it at age three, four, or by the time the child entered school at age five. Several parents were advised by the school there was a problem with the behavior their children were displaying. Difficulty in school was most often the factor parents sought treatment for their child's ADHD symptoms. There were reports of difficulty getting along with peers, distractibility and academic failures, as well as aggressive and violent behaviors. Some parents sought treatment on their own believing something was different with their child. The issues reported by the school were also the noted behaviors parents observed, prompting them to seek treatment on their own.

Once parents made the decision to seek treatment and began to access services, they reported several challenges causing a negative treatment experience. Parents spoke about the desperation they felt in finding the right treatment for their child. While all participants had health insurance at the time they sought treatment, one described paying out of pocket to remain with a specific provider who did not accept insurance. When they could no longer afford to pay out of pocket, they ceased treatment. There were stories of counselors terminating treatment remarking they could not help the child, a therapist falling asleep, and a psychiatrist who booked into the evening hours, and patients waited for hours to be seen. The experiences were overwhelmingly filled with negative attributes. In only one parent case was it reported the parent was able to obtain the treatment needed and without any barriers. That was reported by a mom who is a licensed social worker, works with children with mental illness and behavioral disorders, and has considerable background knowledge of ADHD (per her own account). She described having a firm idea of what her child was presenting with and the type of treatment he would do best with; medication. Her experience with the school system was the only one who described a considerably positive, collaborative effort.

One of the challenges, parents found, was getting the right diagnosis. When parents sought treatment from their medical provider, they did not conclude an ADHD diagnosis in the beginning. A few started with Asperger's, or Autism, then moved into a diagnosis of Sensory Processing Disorder, or was told there was nothing wrong with their children. Parents tried to understand their child's symptoms by seeking a proper diagnosis, however there was not always an immediate resolution. Parents questioned the diagnosis in some cases, once it was given, believing a comprehensive evaluation was not performed for a viable conclusion their children had ADHD. One mother described her pediatrician saying she did not see anything wrong with the boy, but would write a script that he had ADHD so the mother could get additional supportive services for him in school. The mother said she started the medication, but was told she did not have to give it to her son on the weekends. The mother later rationalized if she did not have to give it to him on the weekends, then why does she have to give it to him during the week? She reported temporarily stopping the medication for a period soon after.

Five of the 10 participants denied any cultural, religious, or other values played into their outlook on treatment for ADHD. In one case, the mom stated, 'yes, there were factors that played into her outlook and how her personal values wanted her son to be successful.' That value led her to the decision that she would treat the ADHD symptoms with medication, with the given she knew professionally what the main course of treatment was for the diagnosis. Another mom influenced by personal values was the nurse who referred to her medical background. She said she viewed ADHD through the lens of what the research says about it. She noted her husband was influenced by his Catholic upbringing and did not want to have his son diagnosed with ADHD or any diagnosis, for that matter. It was hard for him to accept his child needed additional supports.

Parents were not always direct in answering this question, but would eventually report they were most open to medication, because they experienced positive effects. Eight of the 10 parents said they were most open to medication, one mother said she was open to anything that would help her child, and reported earlier her child was on ADHD medication. , One mother did not believe in treating young children with ADHD medication and selected therapy as the most desirable treatment. Even when the same parents reported having to go through multiple medications, and titrated dosages, they still considered medication as a treatment to which they were most open. Another mom started out by saying she was most open to natural remedies, then later said they have not been effective, and for that reason she is most open to prescription medication, "because that's the only thing that seemed to work." The parent who expressed being conflicted with the use of medication and abruptly stopped for a period, also reported it was the treatment she was most open to because her son reported to her he felt it was helping him.

In three of the 10 cases parents spoke about being encouraged by their children's school system by a teacher who had a positive influence on them. One parent mentioned how a teacher communicated with her to help her son. Her son is in 10th grade (she referenced his 3rd-grade teacher). She recalled this was the only teacher she felt had tried to help her son. When the other parents were asked in what ways they felt supported and/or discouraged by their child's school, they responded by sharing negative experiences related to services not being provided, lack of guidance or resources being offered, resource barriers, being discouraged, and having to advocate for their children. Only one mother focused solely on the positive experience of the school system, describing herself as having felt 'very supported.'

Parents spoke about the social, emotional, and psychological impact regarding their treatment seeking experience. It has been a difficult road for most of the participants. Much of the difficulty was captured in the themes and patterns presented earlier in this paper. The social impact was having minimal socialization for the adults and the children due to behaviors presented by the children and difficulty obtaining childcare, as well as feeling guilty and shame about the child's conduct. One mom spoke about crying often with feelings of being overwhelmed for what she cannot fix with her son. The negative experiences parents felt were a result of the combination of dealing with the child's behavior and having limited social and familial support.

Parents were asked about significant experiences that stuck out for them and responded with great variances. While one parent focused on the difficulty her son had with nightly homework that brought tears to her eyes during the interview, another mom spoke about the hospitalization her son went through that started them down the 'road of peace.' Another mom spoke about finally feeling like she was understood when the diagnosis of ADHD was identified, and yet another mom spoke about anticipating the response from her husband. Each parent was able to share their distinct experiences of what remained committed to their memory of their experiences seeking treatment for their children.

Summary

The research question was "What is the experience of parents in seeking treatment for their child who is diagnosed with attention deficit hyperactivity disorder? Chapter 4 demonstrated how the data was obtained and examined from the ten parent participant responses. Following the conclusion of data collection and analysis, there were three main themes and their subsequent patterns that evolved that answered the research question. The participants shared they had a difficult and often negative experience seeking treatment for their children. An overwhelming majority of parents identified the school system as a significant stressor and spoke about difficulties that ranged from lack of teacher understanding of the disorder to lack of guidance provided by the school and failure to implement federally mandated services through an IEP and/or 504 Accommodation. Parent's experienced stigma from both external and internal forces that shaped their treatment seeking experiences and decisions. Parents often described a lack of social and family supports and this lack directly impacted their social, emotional, and psychological wellbeing. Parents did not settle on one form of treatment, but every participant described using multiple methods of treatment to find which would work best for their child.

The emphasis of Chapter 5 was to present the significant aspects of the study and summarize the research findings. The connection between the literature as presented in the literature review will be discussed as it relates to the research findings. The strengths and limitations will be reviewed and Chapter 5 will conclude with future research recommendations and the presentation of the conclusions.

CHAPTER 5. RESULTS, CONCLUSIONS, AND RECOMMENDATIONS

Introduction

The research question used in this qualitative study was, "What is the experience of parents in seeking treatment for their child who is diagnosed with attention deficit hyperactivity disorder?" There were 10 parent participants in this study who each sought treatment for their child diagnosed with ADHD. Each of the 10 participants provided rich, detailed, and informative descriptions of experiences acquired through individual open-ended interview questions. A free-flowing conversational style of interviewing was used that allowed participants to contribute in their own words allowing themes to present throughout the process. The interviews lasted approximately 40 to 90 minutes with the researcher who asked open-ended, guided, research questions. There was additional data reviewed: report cards, 504 Accommodation,

IEP's, Behavior Intervention Plans, Disciplinary Referrals, and evaluations. To protect the identity of the participants, report cards, 504 Accommodation, IEP's, Behavior Intervention Plans, Disciplinary Referrals, and evaluations will not be included. The following data was transcribed by this researcher to include interviews, field notes, observations, and any changes made during the member checking phase.

Chapter 5 proceeds to present seven key areas of evaluation of the research study. Some of those areas will include an explanation of the study's significance, study's results, conclusions, and limitations. This section allows the researcher to provide an interpretation of the results as they relate to the research question. Identified results are followed by a discussion of the researcher's conclusions regarding the connection between the research findings and literature on the topic. Additional items discussed in this chapter are limitations and flaws within the research study design, future research recommendations, and a summation and rhetorical suggestions of the dissertation.

Summary of the Results

The purpose of this study was to gain deeper insight into the experiences of parents who sought treatment for their children diagnosed with ADHD. This research is significant because it presents information based on personal experiences of those interviewed regarding the phenomena under study. The incidents of childhood ADHD continues to rise in America annually, and many of those parents seek treatment for their children, yet the research available on the treatment seeking experiences are limited (Mychailyszyn, dosReis, & Myers, 2008). The results from this study have potential to fill a gap in existing literature. This research has significant contributions to systems thinking and treatment as it contributes to the knowledge about parents' treatment seeking experience, which is applicable to the field of psychology as it offers direct parental experiences of those who have a child diagnosed with ADHD.

The academic and non-academic literature was reviewed comprehensively as it related to parents seeking treatment for their children diagnosed with ADHD. The literature review provides a wealth of varying articles probing issues quasi-related to personal treatment-seeking experiences, with a dominant emphasis on the experiences of specific types of treatment such as medication management (Hamrin, McCarthy, & Tyson, 2010; Stroh et al., 2008; Taylor et al., 2006). As the literature review was conducted, it became clear there was marginal literature pertaining to the question about parents' experience in seeking treatment for their child diagnosed with ADHD. The researcher performed a detailed review of the available research, then analyzed, evaluated, and synthesized the existing body of knowledge, demonstrating the originality and significance of this research to the psychological community, and research results now offer greater insight into the experience of parents seeking ADHD treatment.

The use of a qualitative case study for this research allowed for added knowledge in the field and depth of knowledge of the direct parental experiential factors as readers learned more about the phenomenon through detailed-rich, descriptive data. Yin (2009) provided a methodical procedure and comprehensive guide for data analysis that moved the researcher from developing descriptions of the cases to examination and then analysis. Yin's (2009) theoretical framework addresses several key factors for ensuring a high-quality analysis: attending to all evidence, addressing possible rival interpretations, focusing on the the most significant components of the case study, and the use of prior expert knowledge. Yin's (2009) model provided detailed procedures for planning design, preparing, collecting data, analyzing, and sharing the results.

The researcher analyzed each case separately following Yin's guide for conducting a within-case analysis to identify patterns, themes, and significant occurrences from the transcribed data. Following the completion of the within-case analysis, a cross-case analysis was conducted using the data from the 10 individual cases. The emergence of themes and patterns began to evolve because of this analysis.

The first theme presented in this study is the persistent school system challenges. The first theme had four repeated patterns. All the participants except for one remarked about the 504 Accommodation not being implemented or offered. The next pattern is school staff lacked training, knowledge, and effective responses to students with ADHD. The third pattern is that school staff provided limited information, resources, and guidance for parents, and lastly the importance of the role of advocacy in ADHD within the school system.

The second theme discovered in the research is the difficulty parents had in their treatment seeking experience. Three patterns emerged. The first pattern was how the effects of stigma affected the treatment seeking experience. The second was the difficulty parents had in navigating systems for ADHD treatment. Finally, a pattern was identified parents using multiple methods of treatment in an attempt to mediate the ADHD symptoms.

The third and final theme revolved around the general lack of support parents felt they received in the process of finding assistance for their child. Two patterns emerged. The first pattern prevalent amongst the parents was the lack of community support and resources. Parents often compared ADHD to Autism and remarked that unlike the Autism community, there were few-to-no available supports for parents with a child with ADHD. Parents who accessed community supports became involved with the Autism community and remarked about the positive results they felt, but conceded the two disorders are different and ADHD is worthy of having its own supportive community and resources. The second pattern was the lack of social and familial support. Parents remarked about prevalent misunderstandings for ADHD diagnosis; their children being viewed as 'bad' and in need of corporal punishment. This sentiment often caused feelings of isolation, self-doubt, and participants' anger.

Discussion of the Results

In this portion of the discussion, the researcher conveys and interprets the research study results as related to the research question. The practical and theoretical implications and meanings of the study will be clearly presented to the reader, along with design flaws, and elements that possibly impacted study results.

The participants in this research study demonstrated a strong commitment to getting their children with ADHD the help they needed. None of the participants stopped at the first or second failed effort to treat their child, but continued through

multiple efforts and treatment modalities to mediate
the ADHD symptoms. Parents' beliefs about ADHD
and ADHD treatment differed, but they were
connected in fortitude to pursue treatment to result in
the most relief. As the researcher began to interpret
the data, it became evident there was a commonality
of a taxing burden most parents felt in the treatment
seeking experience.

The participants discussed the factors in their
decisions to seek treatment for their children. This
was often prompted by school personnel expressing
concerns about the student's behavior and ADHD
symptoms. In a few cases, parents initiated the
treatment seeking, because they were concerned
about their child's overall functioning behavior.
Parents spoke about their experience in seeking
treatment with nine out of ten participants describing
the negative attributes. When discussing the greatest
challenges and barriers to seek treatment, parents
described a variety of issues faced with from the
school system to not having a proper diagnosis, and
lack of treatment options. Half of the parents denied
any cultural, religious, or other values played into their
outlook on ADHD treatment. Parents discussed the

treatment to which they are most open and many identified medication management because they have seen positive results. Two of the parents, who were initially and adamantly against medication, spoke about the positive influence they saw in their children after starting medication that softened their views on ADHD medication treatment.

The main pattern in the study was the difficulty parents had with interfacing with their school system and in particular that 504 Accommodation were not being implemented or offered to their children with ADHD diagnoses. The prevalence of children not receiving mandated 504 Accommodation was startling given the concept behind the 504 Accommodation is to level the playing field and give children with disabilities the supports they need to achieve the optimal level of success. In the case of the only mother who reported she had a positive experience with her school; she also shared when she directly asked if her son should be given a 504 Accommodation, the teachers quickly dismissed the notion stating it was not necessary. Other parents reported egregious actions of noncompliance from students not being given the testing modifications to others not receiving counseling services. For the child who was not receiving counseling, the mother stated she spoke to the counselor once to inform her and a second time when she was only giving the child group counseling opposed to the group and individual counseling outlined in the 504 Accommodation plan.

Children with ADHD are vulnerable to academic failures resulting from nuances with the disorder. For this reason, ADHD is a qualifying disability under a 504 Accommodation for which these children could have benefitted. One approach is for schools to inform parents of what is available to support their child's academic success. The parents in this study described being 'prepared to fight,' to get their children help in school. Parents shared how they were encouraged to close the 504 Accommodation during annual meetings and in one case the mother felt tremendous guilt for agreeing to close her son's 504 Accommodation when he later struggled in the following school year.

There were two patterns that consistently evoked emotional responses from participants. The patterns were discussing their experiences in navigating systems for ADHD treatment and lack of support; primarily related to community support and resources. The navigating systems experience was marred with negative stories and metaphors used to describe their ordeal. During this question, some of the participants cried, teared up, and/or became visibly angry as they recalled their experiences. One mom questioned how is it that everyone acts as though this never happened before, yet ADHD is a common childhood disorder. The experience of navigating systems was difficult, but not having community supports and resources only compounded the issue. Parents were not able to obtain support specific to ADHD, but alternatively accessed groups established for children with Autism. This pattern of lack of ADHD community resources was persistent in all participants' experiences. Some spoke about finding groups years later that have helped them pertaining to mental illness, but again not specifically ADHD support groups.

Theoretical Implications

Research on the topic of ADHD has evolved from viewing the disorder as an exclusive behavior disorder that is neurologically based (Bailey & Owens, 2005). ADHD can be described with symptoms of inattention, hyperactivity, and impulsivity. While some children may meet the criteria for ADHD with inattention, others may meet criteria for hyperactivity and impulsivity. For students who demonstrate the specified behaviors in both categories, they would receive a diagnosis of ADHD Combined Type. The ADHD disorder affects 5% of children - internationally - regardless of ethnic group or culture (American Psychiatric Association, 2013). As research has shifted from viewing ADHD from a predominant behavioral lens and one of a neurological, it has encompassed findings associated with executive function and its impact on those affected by ADHD. Executive function is located in the brain and responsible for many areas of functioning from working memory, initiation, motivation, planning, and behavior (Barkley et al., 2000). This study demonstrates Barkley's theory on executive function and self-regulation – all the children discussed in this study were diagnosed by a medical doctor with ADHD, through interviews, and review of documents provided by parents, and had sustained impairment in the area of executive function. Some parents provided evaluations used for the Committee on Special Education (CSE) meetings that illustrated the deficits, while others described academic struggles commonly associated with executive dysfunction. To meet the criteria of ADHD one must endorse the symptoms in childhood, but the symptoms have been found to be present throughout the lifespan (American Psychiatric Association, 2013).

The symptomology of Barkley's theory on executive function and self-regulation describes the commonly endorsed symptoms of those who meet criteria for ADHD. Children with ADHD often endorse symptoms related to poor self-regulation as a result of impaired executive function and ADHD has been described as a problem of self- regulation (Hathaway & Barkley, 2003). Children with ADHD also express deficits in the areas of non-verbal working memory and emotional self-regulation as in the case of those affected by executive dysfunction (Alderson, Kasper, Hudec, & Connor, 2013). Some theorists have argued that ADHD is more of an issue of executive function than that of inattention, impulsivity, and in some cases hyperactivity (Barkley & Murphy, 2010). There is a high comorbidity rate with individuals affected by ADHD and other mental health disorders. Some of the comorbidity amongst this diagnosis is oppositional defiant disorder, conduct disorder, anxiety, depression, and learning disabilities (Bailey & Owens, 2005). ADHD and oppositional defiant disorder are two of the most common disorders in childhood and tend to co-occur frequently (Harvey, Breaux, & Lugo-Candelas, 2016). There are a number of impairments associated with the disorder found in childhood and into adulthood such as impaired academics, conduct problems, accident risk, conflictual peer relationships, and poor parent-child relationships (Chen et al., 2008). The presence of ADHD into adulthood has been shown to have the following negative psycho-social outcomes: a decrease of graduation rates, lower grade point averages in college, increased relational and marital conflicts, elevated divorce rates, and a decrease in socio-economic status in comparison with their non-ADHD counterparts (Alderson et al., 2013). These findings only reinforce the need to apply effective treatments in children diagnosed with ADHD to minimize the negative impact across the lifespan. The findings in the

research study aligned with those findings of Barkley
(2010) regarding the neuro-behavioral patterns.

The theoretical overview of Barkley's executive
function and self-regulation theory on ADHD, along
with social stigma, and parental motivation are the
constructs found in the literature regarding the
theoretical model used in this dissertation. Each of the
three theories directly affects one another as they
develop the theoretical framework of the experiences
of parents seeking treatment for their children
diagnosed with ADHD. Barkley's model shifts from the
generally accepted beliefs of ADHD as a
predominantly behavior disorder to one that
encompasses the neurologically-based disorder as
one affecting the brain, and the inability to regulate
behaviors. The executive function in the brain
operates as the key component used for enabling one
to function efficiently in daily living and problem-
solving as one moves towards completing a goal
(Barkley, 2006). Self-regulation allows one to modify
behavior to complete a goal or avoid consequences
for adverse behaviors (Barkley, 2006). Stigma theory
speaks to the various types of stigma that is often
culturally constructed, viewed as a persistent

environmental stressor, and has the ability to cause
the individual to internalize public stigma; self-stigma
(Corrigan & Shapiro, 2010). Parental motivation has a
strong relationship with stigma as it relates to
treatment seeking behaviors and in one study showed
favorable parent motivation outcomes when school
systems partnered with families in treating ADHD
(Hervey-Jumper et al., 2006). The experiences
described by parents in this study support the findings
of Barkley, social stigma, and parental motivation
theories (Corrigan & Shapiro, 2010; Hervey-Jumper et
al., 2006; Barkley, 2006). This researcher believes the
three outlined theories are integrative in their
theoretical applications, and this study corresponds
with these studies.

Practical Implications

The results of this study may provide practical
implications for change in education policy and
practice within that area and the human services field.
Change may be implicated resulting from the theme
of persistent school system challenges. The
researcher suggests that schools do a better job of

informing staff their federal obligations as outlined in federal law specific to the 504 Accommodation. This would mean staff are provided professional development of what a 504 Accommodation entails, the legal mandates under the law, and who qualifies for consideration, which would include students with ADHD. The 504 Accommodation teams may have additional, more comprehensive training to understand their roles, expectations of the meetings, and knowledge about accommodations to consider for those meetings. Meetings could be conducted as outlined by state and federal law and the rights of the parents including communications verbally and in writing. Schools may establish a point person identified for parents to reach out to with any questions regarding the process or their rights under the law.

It may prove helpful for schools to assess students with ADHD and refer them for the 504 Accommodation without waiting for parents to request it and parent advocates to fight for it. Schools could have an internal communication system within their district to inform teachers annually of students with a 504 Accommodation. A written plan for disseminating

504 Accommodation information may be kept on file in the school's main office and provided to every new teacher during onboarding orientation. Too often participants expressed the frustration of having to inform teachers their child had a 504 Accommodation from a previous year not being implemented in the new school year. This cost educational time where students could have been receiving accommodations and lack of the same contributed to their child's academic failures, because support was not in place.

School staff need training and increased knowledge about ADHD. There could be education provided to teachers of the etiology, symptoms, and research-based interventions that work with children with ADHD. Teachers often spend more waking hours with students than the student's parents, and have potential of making a significant difference in the lives of students – specifically children with ADHD. ADHD is one of the main referrals to mental health providers and teachers who have access to such children each school day would benefit from deepening their understanding of the disorder (Chen et al., 2008). The teachers' lack of knowledge influenced the parental experience of treatment seeking while influencing frustration and the disconnect between home and school. One mother spoke about how her child was viewed as 'the bad one,' because the student did not raise her hand to speak and often interrupted others which are classic signs of ADHD. All school staff from bus drivers, monitors, teaching assistants, and administrators, could be required to take competencies courses on ADHD during their tenure, but more specifically within the first year of their education career.

Schools primarily have a captive audience when considering the best measures to provide information and resources to parents. As discussed earlier, it is often the school system initially informing parents of a child's behavioral difficulties. Those discussions often precede parents accessing treatment services. Schools could have resources on the subject of ADHD and information to share with parents. Participants overwhelmingly spoke about the lack of guidance and direction provided by school systems. Schools informed the parents of the behavioral problems, but stopped short of suggesting solutions. Parents described feelings of being frustrated, overwhelmed, and isolated.

All the participants described the negative experiences they had in seeking treatment for their children with an exception of one participant. There were factors presented that influenced these experiences; stigma, navigating systems for ADHD treatment, and the use of multiple treatment methods to resolve the symptoms. There continues to be a need for efforts to reduce ADHD stigma and ADHD treatment stigma. Stigma largely influenced parents, and even in cases with no identifiable outside influences; it was self-stigma that deterred parents from seeking treatment or specific treatment modalities such as medication management. One mom struggled in her response, stating she did not want her son to be on medication, but she saw the positive results and heard positive feedback from him, and therefore, allowed her child to continue taking the medication as prescribed. Those in the human services field should expand their compassion for parents of ADHD children, as they have often attempted many treatment modalities to mediate the symptoms. A parent spoke about feeling judged by the doctor, because they had tried other remedies and were now presenting for medication treatment, while others reported they felt pushed to put their children on medication without being given alternatives. Participants expressed internal struggles about the diagnosis and treatment of ADHD. It is not an easy decision and some compassion and attempts to understand the struggle both external and internal could help to reduce stigma, shame, and self-doubt.

The lack of support was evidently pervasive across all ten cases. In cases where there was evidence of familial support, the parent lacked community support and resources. Making support groups available for parents specific to ADHD will fill a needed gap support. As participants shared their experience, they described having no available resources for ADHD, but found an abundance of parents with children diagnosed with Autism. Some of the participants engaged in the Autism support groups and communities, but felt their situations and needs were different. They concluded they desired support specific to the ADHD experience. Within each community, there could be support provided to families with a child diagnosed with ADHD, where they can engage with others with like issues, and be provided with resources to help their children improve in their overall social, emotional, and behavioral functioning.

This researcher found nothing within the literature review that conflicted with this study's findings. There are no additional articles or published studies this researcher is aware of published during the time-period this study was completed to corroborate or disprove these findings. The findings remained consistent with the early literature review conducted, the theoretical framework and definitions, commonly noted implications, and health care. The research conclusions illustrated ADHD had been previously studied using multiple theoretical frameworks, and spanning a number of academic disciplines (Barkley, 2010; Corrigan & Shapiro, 2010; Hervey-Jumper et al., 2006). Despite the prevalence of ADHD inquiry, there was no research found on the experiences of parents in seeking treatment for their children diagnosed with ADHD.

The limitations mentioned here will be presented briefly as the scope of limitations will be presented fully later in the dissertation. Sample size (n=10) was the first limitation in this study. Although there are many benefits from using a qualitative methodology, it has a significantly lower participant base and makes it difficult to generalize the results to larger populations (Yin, 2009). The second possible limitation is the geographic location of participants as they all came from the same county within the Northeast region of the United States. The third possible limitation was the dependence on participants being honest about their treatment seeking experiences and the ability to recall those experiences accurately. Another possible factor to impact the findings may be that all participants self-identified as Caucasian. It is possible participants from other races and ethnicities may have a different experience in seeking treatment.

The following section will allow the researcher to relate and interpret the results of the study as it relates to the research questions. The practical and theoretical implications, and meanings of the study will elaborate on limitations of the study, design flaws, and any influential factors impacting the results.

The participants in this study shared the common experience of having a child with ADHD and seeking treatment for that child. Many of the parents discussed the difficulty in getting family, friends, and others to understand the difficulty in obtaining the right treatment for their child. This difficulty raised parental emotional distress, frustration, isolation, and anger. Some parents shared that family insisted they use corporal punishment with the child to eliminate the behaviors. Participants in each case described strong responses towards others who made such suggestions and often terminated ties with such individuals. As the researcher began to interpret the data, it was evident why such strong responses were held by the participants. At some point throughout the interviews, participants shared specifically what the symptomology of their child's ADHD symptoms entailed. It was not simply hyperactivity parents encountered, but oppositional behaviors, physically aggressive behaviors in need of physical restraints, nightly struggles with homework, impaired sleep, emotional outbursts, few to no social outlets, and limited supports to help them with the daily struggles. The ongoing difficulties with homework were described by many, yet no one had homework covered under a 504 Accommodation during the time period parents described. Instead, children struggled nightly, and the parents described helping the best they could but it seemed they were the ones who ended up doing the homework and other assignments for their children. Obtaining child care other than for work was an issue in most cases when the children were young, leaving no reprieve for the primary caregiver. The parents stayed vigilant in ensuring the children were taking medication, the child's teachers were aware of the 504 Accommodation, they were prepared to advocate for their child's needs, and they had the strength needed to go to work each day. All the parents were employed, except for one who was on disability, and being supported by her spouse.

The participants shared the factors that went into their decision to seek treatment for their child's ADHD symptoms with many of them reporting the complaints from the school about the child's behaviors, or informing them of academic failure was the main factor, while a couple of the other parents reported they felt there was something not right with their child. The majority of the parents started their quest for treatment at the pediatrician then in some cases progressed to the neurologist where the diagnosis was given. The neurologists were regarded as giving the most comprehensive evaluation for determining the ADHD diagnosis. Not everyone was eager to seek treatment upon being informed of the issues by the school. Some battled their own (stigma) issues of not wanting their child to be different, having to take medication, or conflict within the marital relationship on the best course of action. Some participants spoke about therapists who fired them, stating they cannot help their child, pediatricians who listened and took the time with them, to other practitioners who did not listen and pushed for medication. The treatment regimen that parents were most open to was medication. Even in cases where parents began their answer stating how they do not believe or agree with medication, they concluded it was the one treatment they were most open to because they saw the effectiveness.

The main pattern that evolved was nine participants experienced a difficult treatment seeking experience and one participant reported a favorable experience. There is a need of ADHD support groups; parents need support in parenting a child with ADHD; and parents need resources and information on strategies to help themselves. Parents need education about what resources are available in their

community or neighboring communities. In the case of
these participants, their frustration and isolation was a
direct result of lack of services and supports within
their community for parents of children with ADHD.
The school system in nine cases was listed as a
source of contention where a principal asked a child
to stay home for two weeks, others were not offered
school-based services including a 504
Accommodation, others who had 504's all spoke
about having to fight for those accommodations and
still not having the services provided. This researcher
does question why schools who purport to be
knowledgeable on 504 Accommodation and
interventions for disruptive behaviors are not more
actively informing parents and implementing 504's
when and where applicable. Where are the
professional ethics as they relate to doing what is in
the best interest of the children? Students continue to
act out behaviorally; fail academically, yet there is not
an inquiry as to the best practices for treating
students with ADHD in schools. One mother stated
her issue with the school was her child presumably
was the first student to ever present AHDD behavior.
For that reason, the school offered no help, support,

or aid, but rather the principal asked she keep her child home for two weeks. Over the two weeks mandated suspension, nothing was provided for her son, and when he returned he continued with the behaviors, and subsequently was sent home some days, and suspended on others, in elementary school. The results of the patterns and themes presented in this section were used to form the conclusions that will be discussed next.

Discussion of the Conclusions

In this section, the discussion of the conclusions, the researcher presents conclusions about the relationship of the findings of the study. There was a compare and contrast of the study's findings with the previous understandings, research, and theory in the literature. The children's behaviors described by their parents coincided with Barkley's research (2006), whom found children diagnosed with ADHD have deficits in the executive function areas of their brains, and often demonstrate poor self-regulation; poor working memory, emotional control, initiation, motivation, planning, and behavior. The parents in this study described the same behaviors noted in their children with ADHD. The parents described their children as having a number of academic difficulties resulting in grade retention, meeting criteria for special education due to learning disabilities, and needing accommodations through a 504 Accommodation to help meet the school's educational responsibilities. The parents in this study described their children as having difficulty retaining information, an inability to calm themselves down, no motivation outside of a select few interests like video games, and tremendous difficulty starting a task, which parallels Barkley's (2006) research findings.

Executive function is strongly influenced by difficulties with attention and distractibility, causing impairment in the ability to process information rapidly and with accuracy (Semrud-Clikeman, Walkowiak, Wilkinson, & Butcher, 2010). The literature on executive function and ADHD found the most consistently profound deficits experienced across cases were deficits in vigilance, working memory, response inhibition, and planning (Semrud-Clikeman et al., 2010). Executive function is not solely specific to learning but also impacts one's ability to regulate behavior, note social cues, and how one interprets life events. Semrud-Clikeman et al. (2010) corroborated Barkley's (2006) findings in their meta-analysis of executive function behavior, and agreed working memory was consistently problematic in ADHD and further stated response inhibition is problematic, as well. Response inhibition is often what causes children with ADHD to get into trouble in school, because they lack the ability to stop one task and switch to another effectively. There is a gap in understanding for those with ADHD, when one response is no longer needed and to shift to a new one; to be goal directed. These are the children who have difficulties with transitions because they are not able to modulate from one activity to the next, or insist on completing a task fully before moving on. Each of the participants presented data, either through interviews or data provided relating to psychiatric or neurological evaluations, Individualized Education Plans, or psychological testing, their children experienced the symptoms outlined by Semrud-Clikeman et al. (2010) relative to the impact of executive function on self-regulation, and working memory.

This research agrees with the research of dosReis, Barksdale, Sherman, Maloney, and Charach (2010) who explained parents are often influenced by stigma in their ADHD decision-making process. The social phenomenon of stigma encompasses labeling, discrimination, loss of status, stereotyping, and exclusion (dosReis et al., 2010). This mirrored the descriptions of participants as they shared experiences of 'feeling judged' as parents, having their children excluded from social functions, and parental fear of stigma-type labels from doctors, schools, and society. There has been research related to treatment seeking among individuals with ADHD that has shown social stigma was a strong contributing factor for preventing treatment. The stigmatizing beliefs, overmedicating children for behavioral disorders, and long term developmental effects on children who accept medication, are negative perspectives serving as barriers, as they influence parental treatment-seeking behaviors (dosReis et al., 2010). This connects with the participants' descriptions of how stigma influenced their treatment-seeking journey. There were several parents who spoke about how stigma influenced their contempt for the use of medication. Some parents felt it was viewed as the easy way out, while others said they did not want to consider the physical effects the medication would cause, or how they would be viewed by others. Self-stigma was considerable among parents who experienced stigma, as they questioned their abilities to make proper decisions, and blamed themselves for their child's disorder.

There are various contributing factors to motivation that were found in the literature that included parent behavior training, culture, school systems, and stigma (Arcia & Fernandez, 1998; Fabiano, 2007; Hervey-Jumper et al., 2006; Peters & Jackson, 2009). Fabiano (2007) discussed a commonly recommended treatment for ADHD; parent behavior training (BPT). The purpose of BPT's are to provide parents with psycho-education about responding to triggers, responding appropriately with consequences, and targeting adverse behaviors (Fabiano, 2007). There was one parent who said she repeatedly heard about parent training, but she dismissed those suggestions and focused on the physiological aspects of brain chemistry in the ADHD disorder. She did not feel that BPT would work for her because that training would not change what was going on within her son. The majority of the participants' spoke about the need for training, resources, and information on how to help their children with ADHD. One mom asked the research for someone to give her the answers, tell her what she is supposed to do, and guide her in parenting her daughter with ADHD.

This research also agreed with the research of Hervey-Jumper, Douyon, and Franco (2006) who found a direct correlation between a parents' perception of the school as unhelpful, their hesitancy to accept the diagnosis, and utilization of a medication treatment regimen. This paralleled what parents described in their responses to the school that informed them of behavioral concerns with their children. Some parents remarked about feeling the school, and specifically teachers, were not doing everything possible to help their child. They described staff 'set off' their children, did not provide mandated supports, viewed their child as lacking motivation, and being "bad." In cases where the parents felt the teachers were not supportive, they were less accepting of the ADHD diagnosis. Some parents spoke about how they were not going to accept medication treatment to make the teachers' jobs easier. In contrast, the mother who had a positive school experience reported she accepted the ADHD when her son continued to struggle in school academically and was receptive to medication as the sole treatment response upon being diagnosed. This mom was a social worker, who shared her background knowledge on ADHD and recommended treatments. In the case of a mom of an 11-year-old, she accepted medication treatment following the comments of a teacher whom she felt was supporting her son through his academic failures and behavioral challenges. To improve the outcomes for children with ADHD, it is essential to building a positive trust between parents and teachers (Hervey-Jumper et al., 2006).

Chen and Johnston (2007) stated ADHD had a high comorbidity rate with other disorders along with many other impairments in daily living, such as the risk of accidents, social acceptance, and impaired parental relationships. Their study explored how gender affects parental beliefs of ADHD symptoms. They reviewed a variety of areas of the child's life.

This research study coincided with Chen, Seipp, and Johnston's (2008) research children with ADHD have a high comorbidity rate with other disorders; there are significant impairments in daily living, limited social acceptance, and parental conflict. Seven of the 10 participants reported their children had been diagnosed with a comorbid disorder along with ADHD. Some of the comorbidity included learning disabilities, Autism, Oppositional Defiant Disorder, Tourette's, Sensory Processing Disorder (SPD), Asperger's, and Anxiety Disorder. All participants shared difficulties their children have in managing themselves with daily living activities especially in organization. Some used checklists to assist with getting ready for school and out of the house to meet the bus. Others incorporated lists into the school day to remind children what books needed to be brought to the next class and home for the day. Other moms described having a family calendar where all activities, sports, and appointments are placed on it so the child will be able to see what is coming up in the next days and weeks. This study supported earlier research of impaired parental relationships among children with ADHD. Nine participants described the relationship difficulties

as they attempted to provide support for their child –
not always well received. Parents described
arguments over behavior, the child's aggressive
relationships with their siblings, lack of motivation,
nightly homework, and the symptoms associated with
ADHD (hyperactivity, impulsivity, and inattention).
Some parents with older children described trying to
set limits their AHDD child consistently overstepped.
As those parents spoke, one could hear the
weariness in their voices as they described not
knowing what to do to make their child follow their
rules, while at the same time expressing the many
efforts they made to enforce them.

This research also supports Chen, Seipp, and
Johnston's (2008) research as it relates to social
acceptance. This part of the interview consistently
changed the way parents told their stories. One could
hear the pain in their voices as they sometimes
described very isolative social lives outside and within
the school walls. One mom spoke about how her child
had difficulty with forging peer relationships, "We
never really found a connection to anybody with
whom she formed a relationship." As this same mom
continued through eyes swelling with tears, a lump in

her throat, and hesitation in her voice, she continued her story. Her daughter expressed to her, "I don't feel like I fit in. I don't have friends." She spoke about asking her child whom she sits with at lunch. The child responded with the name of the classmate she sits next to, "... but we don't talk." This mom said she observed how other children in the class have forged relationships because they have been in the same cohort group for four years, but her daughter 'never really had birthday parties with other kids, no sleepovers, no play dates.' This part of the interview was the most emotionally difficult for this mom as she pushed past tears to share her story. Other parents shared similar experiences where they felt there was not enough understanding or acceptance of their child's diagnosis. Some parents specifically involved their children in sports to mediate these social issues. They also observed in most cases that despite extracurricular involvement, that activity did little to foster the strong social bonds the parents aimed to achieve.

Kaufman and Nuerk (2008) reported there is a high comorbidity rate with ADHD and learning disabilities that are around 9 to 25%. The article by

Kaufman and Nuerk (2008) discussed the prevalence of academic challenges among children with ADHD that coincides with the findings of this research study. Nine of the participants either had a 504 Accommodation, or an Individualized Education Plan (IEP). The one parent who reported she did not have either, stated when she asked if her son should be considered for a 504 Accommodation, the school replied that 'would not be necessary.' The researcher reviewed data provided by participants that included meeting notes from 504's and IEP's. That data outlined the academic challenges and deficiencies of student performance. Two areas often found to be impacted in children with ADHD is working memory and listening comprehension (McInnes, Humphries, Hogg-Johnson, & Tannock, 2003). Working memory allows the temporary storage and manipulation of information vital for complex cognitive tasks such as comprehension, learning, and reasoning (Martinussen & Major, 2011). Working memory ties into Barkley's theory on ADHD and executive function described earlier. This pattern was also noted among the data submitted for review. The findings by Kaufman and Nuerk (2007) emphasized that inhibitory deficiencies seem to be a key factor in ADHD children, as well as indicates impact of different task requirements on the performance of cognition.

The research presented by Pellow, Solomon, and Barnard (2011) paralleled this research as they demonstrated more parents were seeking complementary and alternative medical therapies (CAM). Traditional forms of treatment are still being utilized and include medication, behavioral management, and school-based treatment such as accommodations to support student success (Pellow et al., 2011). This research showed parents used many different treatment modalities to mediate their child's ADHD symptoms. The participants all reported using multiple methods even when they found one that helped their child. As they described, it was often through trial-and-error they found an intervention that worked for their child. Parents all reported using some, or all, of the traditional methods stated by Pellow et al. (2011). They further expressed a wide range of complementary alternative medical therapies. Some of the alternative treatments being sought by parents are diet, exercise therapy, supplemental interventions, herbal and homeopathic treatment (Pellow et al., 2011). In this study, parents described the use of diet restriction, herbal medicine, the Feingold diet, restriction of red dye number 40, removing preservatives, and natural homeopathic. Similar to factors discussed by Pellow et al., (2011), the parents in this study discussed their concerns over the use of medication treatment and for this reason chose to try other avenues.

Despite there being a wealth of research on the topic of ADHD, there are gaps in the research surrounding school-based functioning, interventions, and assessments (DuPaul & Jimerson, 2014). One of the areas DuPaul and Jimerson (2014) focused on in their study, was examining the degree that school intervention plans were including recommended best practices and evidence-based research. In this study, parents described having the 504 Accommodation not being implemented. That is one concern warranting attention. The other concern as presented in this article is the types of accommodations being offered. The researcher did not find research during the literature review that spoke to the significant concerns presented by participants: mandated services are not being provided. When searching the literature following the development of this pattern within the study, the researcher found articles related to best practices when developing a 504 Accommodation. This pattern of understanding what reasons contribute to the lack of implementation of 504's may be worthy of future research.

School teachers play a significant role in the lives of children with ADHD, especially in the identification of behavioral, social, or academic concerns. Weyandt, Fulton, Schepman, Verdi, and Wilson (2009) conducted research examining the knowledge of teachers and school psychologists. This study coincides with the research of Weyandt et al. (2009) as participants spoke about encountering teachers who were not knowledgeable about the disorder, and, therefore, the interventions were not effective in addressing the ADHD symptoms of concern. Weyandt et al. (2009) found many myths still abound concerning the etiology of ADHD that include misattributing ADHD to poor diet (food coloring, preservatives), too much natural or processed sugars, fluorescent lighting, soaps and detergents, excessive yeast, tar and pitch exposure, insect repellants, deficient teaching styles, and environmental pollutants

(Weyandat et al., 2009). When one believes there is a certain cause of origin for a disorder, intervention strategies will align with that cause. This is where the breakdown between the presentation of ADHD symptoms and the school response occurs. Weyandt et al. (2009) found that strategies are being used based on such myths that are not empirically validated to treat ADHD. Participants spoke about their children being suspended, one kindergarten student was asked to remain home for two weeks, others were sent to the principal's office, parents were called, and others asked to pick their child up early. Parental frustration grew from the lack of preventive measures happening for their child in school. The children were disciplined because of their behavior, but not provided the tools, or supports to change their behaviors, as described by parents. This study supports the findings of this research as it illustrates the impact of lack of teacher knowledge and offers a number of empirically validated strategies that have been proven to work with children with ADHD: incorporating action-oriented tasks that require student's active response, continual feedback, clear instructions, highly structured educational tasks, adding color to text to stimulate materials, and reducing lengthy assignments by chucking them into smaller parts (Weyandt et al., 2009). These empirically validated interventions are a small scope of what has been included in research to be effective in working with students with ADHD in the school setting.

This section provided a comparative and contrasting look at the study's findings and literature. This study is supported in a multitude of areas from the influence of stigma, parental motivation, and the role of executive function, to social acceptance, comorbidity, and school challenges. The next section will discuss the limitations of this research study.

Lessons Learned

The first lesson learned is school systems are the single most significant stressor that parents encounter in their quest for treatment for their children's ADHD symptoms. It is often the school informing the parents of the concerns and at the same time, the school system which repeatedly, across cases, withheld mandated services that these children were eligible to receive. In other cases, parents were not informed that their children could receive a 504 Accommodation and they continued to struggle academically and behaviorally. Teachers are not knowledgeable enough about the disorder nor about best practices in treating ADHD in a school setting. This led to parents who felt blamed, like they were a burden, and their needs were not heard. Some of the parents who were able to identify a teacher who made a positive impact on them also shared that teachers had informed them of their rights under a 504 Accommodation or IEP. Three parents clearly expressed their beliefs that teachers were not allowed to provide parents with resource information the parents needed, whether that was due to restraints or finances.

The second lesson learned is there is a gap in services within the community for parents with children diagnosed with ADHD. Parents were able to identify support groups and programs for children with Autism and found such groups helpful. The needs of the children vary and this lack of connection to supports and resources left parents feeling isolated in the treatment seeking process. Parents found resources (information) suggesting the best way to address their child's ADHD symptoms were unavailable, causing increased frustration, and being overwhelmed (emotional feelings) with the process.

The third lesson is, that as much as the mental health community has made efforts to decrease stigma and raise awareness, ADHD continues to need additional efforts in raising awareness. The stigmatizing pressure influenced parent's treatment-seeking decisions and thus their experiences. When there were no external stigmatizing forces parents' sometimes engaged in internalized stigma. Despite the direction the stigma was led from it fostered blame, self-doubt, and questioning of one's parenting abilities.

The fourth lesson clearly demonstrates the overall experience of parents seeking treatment is marred with difficulties. Parents spoke about not knowing the best course of treatment and relying on others who specialize in working with children, such as school staff, and not receiving any direction or guidance of where they can go for help and what they can do as parents. Parents described feeling like they were out there on their own and fought a losing battle.

Their analogies expressed the level of desperation they felt in trying to get their children the help they needed.

Another lesson learned is the lack of social and familial support parents had. It is difficult to obtain childcare, family members who do not have children with the disorder do not fully understand, and others often gave advice the child needed corporal punishment to address the behavioral issues. These comments from friends and others often drew a relationship wedge between parents and others and impacted their social, emotional, and psychological health. One mom spoke about crying more, once her child got into school than she ever cried, because he had daily difficulties with his behavior.

This study demonstrated all parents used multiple methods of treatment in hopes of mediating the ADHD symptoms. Accepting medication management was difficult for most and the (best) accepted treatment for a few. Even in cases where prescription medication was used, parents still attempted other treatments including herbal remedies, behavior modifications to psychiatric evaluations, counseling, and change of diet.

Finally, in all cases, the parents described seeing atypical behaviors early, in some cases believing it was the 'terrible twos.' When their child's behaviors got progressively worse as they entered the school system, parents began to question if it could be something more. Some parents reported having evaluations performed by age three or shortly thereafter to gain insight into the presenting issues.

Limitations

Each qualitative study is accompanied by its own set of limitations. This study contained a sample size (n=10), which posed our first limitation. Case studies often have a smaller sample size than its quantitative counterpart. For this reason, it is difficult to generalize the findings in this study to a larger population. Yin (2009) discussed the benefits in using a qualitative methodology while acknowledging the significantly lower participant base, it is difficult to generalize the results to larger populations. Data saturation is reached once the development of new patterns or themes cease; data saturation was met in this study upon the conclusion of the ninth interview. This researcher chose to obtain one additional participant to ensure saturation was met. It is beneficial to have a larger sample whenever feasible to generalize the study's findings as much as possible, beyond the immediate sample under study.

The second possible limitation is the geographic location of participants as they all came from the same county within the Northeastern region of the United States. There was a limitation in the analysis of the small sample size (*n*=10) that included participants from one northeastern county. For this reason, the findings may not be generalizable to other counties or states across the United States or outside of this country. Services, especially human services, can vary greatly from one county to the next county, within the same state. Undoubtedly there will be differences across states regarding the services provided, the acceptance of seeking treatment, the barriers that may be posed, and other influential factors. One county in an urban city with mass transportation and easier access to healthcare services may differ from a much rural county where lack of transportation leads to lack of involvement in healthcare services. It could be argued those living in the same county will have similar experiences than those living outside of that specific county. Having the ability to engage a larger geographic sample could enhance the transferability of this research study. The ability to replicate this study with a larger sample is possible, or in other parts of the country, or other countries where children are diagnosed with ADHD. Case studies have a valuable place within the research community, however because of the nature of the design, such as sample size, it is difficult to replicate.

The third potential limitation was the dependence on participants being honest about their treatment seeking experiences and the ability to recall those experiences accurately. Researcher reactivity is when participants will tell a researcher what they believe is the 'right' answer instead of their own personal truth. This is often done to appease the researcher for a variety of reasons and, therefore, can pose limitations within a study. In any study, it is necessary for participants to be able to recall the information they are sharing for it to provide insight into the truths of their personal experiences. It was helpful for parents to share their data with the researcher. This process assisted in verifying information of dates, time-frames, specific classifications, reasons for suspensions, and other helpful information. There were times when parents were observed doing their best to try to recall information to a question asked. During those times, the researcher reminded them, if they were unable to remember information, that it was fine. At other times when participants were attempting to recall, then quickly provided an answer, perhaps due to the uncomfortable silence, this researcher reminded them that it was fine if they didn't remember. If they insisted it was accurate, the researcher took additional time and careful consideration during the analysis of that data. The data provided, helped participants to recall the chronology and nuances of their treatment seeking experiences.

A possible fourth factor to impact the findings may be all participants self-identified as Caucasian. Much of the available research on ADHD involving parents, contains a predominance of Caucasian parents. There were recommendations for future research to focus on the experiences of ethnic minorities; African American and Latino. This study was open for parents of all races and ethnicities. All the parents who inquired about the study who met inclusion were Caucasian. There was one father who inquired about the study, but after the fifth of 12 questions were asked, it was determined he did not meet inclusion (did not have a child diagnosed with ADHD). Therefore, his race and ethnicity was unknown and not pertinent once he was excluded from the study. Perhaps there may need to be a study of what factors limit African American and Latino parents' involvement in research studies concerning ADHD. In this study, all 10 participants self-identified as Caucasian, with one of the 10 self-identifying ethnically as Caucasian, Italian, Russian, and Hungarian. It is possible participants from other races and ethnicities may have a different experience in seeking treatment. There are factors that may impact the experiences of parents from other races. Cultural acceptance of treatment seeking, discrimination, socio-economic factors, or incidents of ADHD within a group can all impact the overall treatment seeking experience.

The fifth and final identified potential limitation within this study is researcher bias. A researcher can affect the data in a qualitative study because of the subjective nature of the design, and unknowingly impose observer bias in the analysis, and interpretation of the data. The data could have been affected if researcher bias was included in the data collection, analysis, or any part of the research process. The researcher could influence the interviews by guiding the participants at the onset of the research questions, not allowing them to answer completely, or by only reporting what the findings should be based on personal assumptions. The potential researcher biases stated earlier, included the interactions with parents in a professional manner who reported difficulties in obtaining ADHD treatment, because of their interactions with medical providers. The researcher prepared a plan to address such biases if they arose. Some of the safeguards planned to be implemented in this study include reflexivity, member checking, consulting with mentor, field notes to include reflections of thoughts and feelings towards the process, and developing themes and patterns. The researcher is ethically obligated to reduce any misrepresentation or misunderstandings; as a licensed social worker, this has been a duty of the profession for the 12 years the license has been held.

This topic is a professional one this researcher has engaged with multiple times; children diagnosed with ADHD and parents seeking treatment services. The research findings have the potential to enhance the understanding of parental experiences in seeking treatment for their children diagnosed with ADHD.

Integrity and credibility were important aspects to be maintained in this study. Every effort was made to present each parents" experiences accurately as this is essential in qualitative work (Lietz & Zayas, 2010). One way credibility was built into the research design was through triangulation. There were multiple theoretical schemes, methods, and data sources used to accomplish the goal of building credibility (Creswell, 2013). Data triangulation was used in this study with a variety of data selected by participants to contribute. These documents, participant interviews and participant observations formed the basis of the triangulation of data. Member checking was another way to maintain credibility in this study. Every participant was contacted following the transcription of data, to check for the accuracy of the data analysis to ensure it reflected the participants' experiences. This process was helpful as it aided in the researcher's ability to present accurate information. The audiotapes were strategically positioned to minimize researcher reactivity, biases were discussed with a mentor to increase self-awareness, and a written journal was maintained throughout the research process. In conclusion, of the research efforts, credibility was maintained by the presentation of accurate representations of the research findings.

The participants all came from the same county in a Northeastern state. If it were fiscally possible of this researcher, it would be of interest to see if parents in other states within the United States had the same experiences as the patterns revealed in this study, or if they would produce additional patterns and themes. Accessing parents from ethnicities other than Caucasian may also provide different experiences in parental treatment seeking endeavors. The literature on ADHD and parents has demonstrated a shortage in research including parents who are African American and Hispanic. Research specific to the experiences of these groups may show a varied experience than their Caucasian counterpart. One way to address the potential limitation of parents' ability to recall is to set a time frame from the point of diagnosis to the point of participant recruitment. This research allowed inclusion for any parent who had a child between 5 and 18-years of age. This allowed for a wide scope of parents who are at different stages of their treatment seeking experiences. It allowed for parents of teenagers to describe their experiences over the last ten years or so, which was very beneficial to the purposes of this study. This study was able to capture the longevity of treatment seeking instead of a specific or few encounters.

Recommendations for Future Research or Interventions

The replication of this study would be a recommendation for future research, expand the geographical location, and increase the number of participants involved. By examining parents from other parts of the country, or within other countries, that will serve as a comparative or contrasting study to these findings. One could then probe further into the cultural, national, or other attributes that influence parents in the treatment seeking journey. Another study could research the experiences of African

Americans and Latinos within the United States and gather an understanding of their experiences of seeking treatment. There has been some research published regarding how cultural attributions influenced medication treatment seeking for ADHD, however, research involving ethnic minorities, and various cultural differences has been limited concerning ADHD (Schmitz & Velez, 2003). Future research may uncover specific nuances different ethnicities face in their treatment seeking experience.

A study could be designed involving schools and their responses to ADHD. This study showed the disconnect between the school community and parents. There could be a study that focuses in on identifying what factors impeded a school from providing students with mandated services through a 504 Accommodation or IEP. Taking a closer look at the barriers that school systems face in providing those services could greatly improve the school experience of the child with ADHD.

Continuing with the school system, it was noted in nine of the 10 experiences that parents felt that schools did not provide them with resources or information to benefit their child with ADHD. This researcher supports the findings of Bussing et al. (2007) that additional research is needed on the most effective methods for schools to inform parents of ADHD intervention options. Another area of research could be an experiment where one group of teachers are provided with comprehensive education on the etiology and evidenced-based, best practices for working with children with ADHD, and then measure outcomes of their responses to student behaviors several times throughout the school year. The research would investigate if teachers increase their level of confidence and ability in working with children with ADHD when they have been provided the background knowledge and skills to manage the behaviors.

Lastly, research could involve community-based clinics where children receive ADHD treatment and assess how effective they are in providing parents with information: available community supports, best practices for parenting a child with ADHD, and how parents can effectively respond to the adverse behaviors associated with the disorder. The study would also assess how effective community-based clinics are at informing parents of school-based services such as 504s and special education services. The study would also examine the specific treatment modalities that community-based clinics are using with children diagnosed with ADHD. Parents in this study spoke about the significant lack of knowledge and resources provided to them from all aspects of care. This study would look at how effective the community counseling organizations are at addressing this need, then meaningful recommendations could be made once the gaps in services have been identified.

Conclusion

The research question, "What is the experience of parents in seeking treatment for their child who is diagnosed with Attention Deficit Hyperactivity Disorder?" was the main focus of the research study, literature review, analysis of data, and data synthesis. Three themes and nine patterns emerged from this qualitative case study. The study has met the challenge in answering the research question and as a result, of such has provided a deeper, more meaningful understanding of what parents have experienced.

The participants shared a number of reasons why they initially sought treatment for their child's ADHD, however, the majority of them discussed how it was as a result of the school reporting concerns to them. In a few of the other cases, the parents sought help because the child's behavior was concerning. Some parents spoke about how they thought their child was going through the "terrible two's", and became increasingly concerned when they turned three, then four-years old, and the behavior, and symptoms were progressively worsening. Some parents discussed the hesitation they had in seeking treatment following the teacher's concerns. In those cases, parents eventually followed through when the negative behavioral reports from school continued.

The parents spoke about their experience with seeking treatment and reported various items in response to this question, from the difficulties they faced, to the positives they encountered. The neurologist was most often described as thorough in their evaluation of this disorder, provided information to the parents in verbal and written form, and with whom the parents appeared to have the most respect for. Three parents described their pediatrician and reported a favorable interaction from the physician because they listened, they took the time in assessing for ADHD, and explained the disorder to the parents.

Some of the greatest challenges and barriers to seeking treatment were overwhelmingly with the school system. Discussing the school's interaction with their child's ADHD was one of the most emotional parts of the interviews across the board for most participants. Parents felt there was not enough being done by the school, teachers did not care, and mandated services were not being provided.

Parents discussed the treatment options they were most open to and more often identified, as medication. The one reason parents persistently stated medication was the one treatment to which they were most open was because they said they saw the positive effects. Even parents who reported they had a hard time accepting medication treatment, spoke about how they came to accept the option for their child.

Parents were asked how they felt supported and/or discouraged by their child's school system. A few parents spoke about a teacher who helped them along the way, a specialized program their child was sent to, going to see the school psychologist, and the use of a fidget ball. Parents who spoke about how they were discouraged by their school, reported the items previously mentioned, and having to 'fight' for what their child needed, anger about mandated services not being provided, and no one telling them what they could do to help the situation.

The social, emotional, and psychological impact on parents has been evident as they expressed how managing their child's symptoms are a daily event from which they do not get a break. Finding child care for times other than work was not available for any of the parents. They have diminished social lives resulting in their lack of ability to engage with others inside or outside of their home. Parents reported feeling lonely and isolated, as well as having self-doubt and blame, resulting in their child's diagnosis. Other parents discussed the impact it has made on marital relationships, as well as interactions with extended family and social friendships.

Parents described the significant difficulties they have had in navigating systems to get their child treatment for ADHD. This section provoked the most parental metaphors and visible pain. Even though parent participants used many words to be sure this researcher understood what it was like, they made every effort to expound on descriptions. The researcher understood this process of navigating ADHD systems to be one of isolation, frustration, lacking direction, and emotionally exhausting. Parents shared significant experiences that stood out regarding seeking treatment with varied responses. Some participants spoke more about the school systems and how difficult it was obtaining support and resources.

The researcher hopes the findings of this study will add to and complement existing literature in the area of parental treatment seeking experiences, for practitioners who treat children diagnosed with ADHD, school systems, and communities who have the ability to form organizations and support groups for this population. This research has the possibility of providing new and relevant knowledge about the experience of parents seeking treatment for their children diagnosed with ADHD. Parents have been provided a platform to voice their experiences in seeking treatment.

It is the hope of this researcher that this research will raise awareness as follows:

- Assist practitioners how parents experience the treatment seeking task;
- Encourage school systems to understand how they impact a parents' treatment seeking journey, how to decrease parental isolation, and the importance of providing resources, and mandated services as outlined in the 504 Accommodation and IEP's;
- Enlighten the larger community of the struggle and tremendous burden parents hold in their pursuit of seeking treatment for their child, but also parenting the child with ADHD. Parents should not be judged, or isolated, but instead be supported, and provided resources to enhance outcomes for them and their children.

Ten parents volunteered to participate in this research study, all of whom have a child diagnosed with ADHD they have sought treatment for. They answered questions, and they all were open about their experiences in seeking treatment with the intent they would help others by sharing their stories.

It is the hope of this researcher this study will address the gap in the literature specific to the question of parental experience in seeking treatment. The behaviors of children with ADHD are pervasive and can be physically exhausting for the parent to manage. Additional resources, understanding, and support could make a positive difference in both the children's and parent's lives. Increased support can come from the schools with students with ADHD for a large part of their day, and then from community-based clinics, pediatricians, other practitioners, and the communities at large. Parents and children with ADHD need additional resources and support groups in their communities. This would be helpful in providing parents with the social support they need, providing information, and reducing stigma. This research could be used by practitioners, schools, and the medical community to deepen their understanding of parental treatment seeking experiences and allow these findings to inform their interactions with parents.

REFERENCES

Abikoff, H., Hechtman, L., Klein, R. G., Gallagher, R., Fleiss, K., Etcovitch, J., & Pollack, S. (2004). Social functioning in children with ADHD treated with long-term methylphenidate and multimodal psychosocial treatment. *Journal of the American Academy of Child & Adolescent Psychiatry, 43,* 820–829. doi:10.1097/01.chi.0000128797.91601.1a

Ahmed, R., McCaffery, K. J., & Aslani, P. (2013). Factors influencing parental decision making about stimulant treatment for attention-deficit/hyperactivity disorder. *Journal of Child and Adolescent Psychopharmacology, 23*(3), 163-78. doi:10.1089/cap.2012.0087

Alderson, R. M., Kasper, L. J., Hudec, K. L., & Patros, C. G. (2013). Attention-deficit/hyperactivity disorder (ADHD) and working memory in adults: A meta-analytic review. *Neuropsychology, 27*(3), 287-302. doi:10.1037/a0032371

American Psychiatric Association. (2000). Diagnostic and statistical manual of mental disorders (4th ed., text rev.). Washington, DC: Author.

American Psychiatric Association. (2002). *American psychiatric association practice guideline for the treatment of patients with bipolar disorder.* Arlington, VA: American Psychiatric Publishing.

American Psychiatric Association. (2013). Diagnostic and statistical manual of mental disorders (5th ed.). Arlington, VA: American Psychiatric Publishing.

Arcia, E., & Fernandez, M. C. (1998). Cuban mothers' schemas of ADHD: Development, characteristics, and help seeking behavior. *Journal of Child and Family Studies, 7*(3), 333-352. doi:10.1023/A:1022945628866

Bailey, R. K., & Owens, D. L. (2005). Overcoming challenges in the diagnosis and treatment of attention-deficit/hyperactivity disorder in African Americans. *Journal of the National Medical Association, 97*(10), 5S-10S.

Barkley, R. A. (1997). Behavioral inhibition, sustained attention, and executive functions: constructing a unifying theory of ADHD. *Psychological Bulletin, 121*(1), 65.

Barkley, R. A. (2006). *Attention-Deficit Hyperactivity Disorder: A Handbook for Diagnosis and Treatment* (3rd ed.). New York, NY: Guilford.

Barkley, R. A. (2007). School interventions for attention deficit hyperactivity disorder: Where to from here? *School Psychology Review, 36*(2), 279-286.

Barkley, R. A., & Murphy, K. R. (2010). Impairment in occupational functioning and adult ADHD: The predictive utility of executive (EF) ratings versus EF tests. *Archives of Clinical Neuropsychology, 25*, 157–173. doi:10.1093/arclin/acq014

Barkley, R. A., Shelton, T. L., Crosswait, C., Moorehouse, M., Fletcher, K., Barrett, S., ... Metevia, L. (2000). Multi-method psycho-educational intervention for preschool children with disruptive behavior: Preliminary results at post-treatment. *Journal of Child Psychology and Psychiatry, 41*(03), 319-332.

Barzman, D. H., Fieler, L., & Sallee, F. R. (2004). Attention-deficit hyperactivity disorder: Diagnosis and treatment. *Journal of Legal Medicine, 25*(1), 23-38. Retrieved from EBSCOhost.

Berger-Jenkins, E., McKay, M., Newcorn, J., Bannon, W., & Laraque, D. (2012). Parent medication concerns predict underutilization of mental health services for minority children with ADHD. *Clinical Pediatrics, 51*(1), 65-76. doi:10.1177/0009922811417286

Biederman, J., Faraone, S., & Monuteaux, M. (2002). Impact of exposure to parental attention-deficit hyperactivity disorder on clinical features and dysfunction in the offspring. *Psychological Medicine, 32*, 817–827.

Brinkman, W. B., & Epstein, J. N. (2011). Promoting productive interactions between parents and physicians in the treatment of children with attention-deficit/hyperactivity disorder. *Expert Review of Neurotherapeutics, 11*(4), 579-88. doi: http://dx.doi.org/10.1586/ern.10.151

Brinkman, W. B., Sherman, S. N., Zmitrovich, A. R., Visscher, M. O., Crosby, L. E., Phelan, K. J., & Donovan, E. F. (2009). Parental angst making and revisiting decisions about treatment of attention-deficit/hyperactivity disorder. *Pediatrics, 124*(2), 580-589.

Burns, G., & Walsh, J. A. (2002). The influence of ADHD –

Hyperactivity/Impulsivity symptoms on the development of oppositional defiant disorder symptoms in a 2-year longitudinal study. *Journal of Abnormal Child Psychology, 30,* 245–256.

Bussing, R., Gary, F. A., Mills, T. L., & Garvan, C. (2003). Parental explanatory models of ADHD. *Social Psychiatry & Psychiatric Epidemiology, 38*(10), 563. doi:10.1007/s00127-003-0674-8

Bussing, R., Gary, F., Mills, T., & Garvan, C. (2007). Cultural variations in parental health beliefs, knowledge, and information sources related to attention-deficit/hyperactivity disorder. *Journal of Family Issues, 28*(3), 291-318.

Bussing, R., Zima, B. T., Gary, F. A., & Wilson- Garvan (2003). Barriers to detection, help-seeking, and service use for children with ADHD symptoms. *The Journal of Behavioral Health Services & Research, 30*(2), 176-89.

Charach, A., & Gajaria, A. (2008). Improving psychostimulant adherence in children with ADHD. *Expert Review of Neurotherapeutics, 8*(10), 1563-71. doi: http://dx.doi.org/10.1586/14737175.8.10.1563

Charach, A., Yeung, E., Volpe, T., Goodale, T., & dosReis, S. (2014). Exploring stimulant treatment in ADHD: Narratives of young adolescents and their parents. *BMC Psychiatry, 14,* 110. doi: http://dx.doi.org/10.1186/1471-244X-14-110

Charmaz, K. (2006). *Constructing grounded theory: A practical guide through qualitative analysis.* Thousand Oaks, CA: Sage Publications.

Chen, M., & Johnston, C. (2007). Maternal inattention and impulsivity and parenting behaviors. *Journal of Clinical Child and Adolescent Psychology, 36*(3), 455-468.

Chen, M., Seipp, C. M., & Johnston, C. (2008). Mothers' and fathers' attributions and beliefs in families of girls and boys with attention-deficit/hyperactivity disorder. *Child Psychiatry and Human Development, 39*(1), 85-99. doi: http://dx.doi.org/10.1007/s10578-007-0073-6

Corrigan, P. W., & Shapiro, J. R. (2010). Measuring the impact of programs that challenge the public stigma of mental illness. *Clinical Psychology Review, 30*(8), 907-922.

Creswell, J. W. (2013). *Research design: Qualitative, quantitative, and mixed methods approaches.* Thousand Oaks, CA: Sage Publications.

Demaray, M. K., Elting, J., & Schaefer, K. (2003). Assessment of attention-deficit hyperactivity disorder (ADHD): A comparative evaluation of five, commonly used, published rating scales. *Psychology in the Schools, 40*(4), 341.

Dongil, K., Ienai, K., Sora, J., Jaehyun, S., Jiyoung, A., & Eunyoung, K. (2011). School-based screening of ADHD, LD and comorbid ADHD/LD: The case of an elementary school in Korea. *KEDI Journal of Educational Policy, 8*(1), 143-165.

Dorneles, B. V., Corso, L. V., Costa, A. C., Pisacco, N. M. T., Sperafico, Y. L. S., & Rohde, L. A. P. (2014). The impact of DSM-5 on the diagnosis of learning disorder in ADHD children and adolescents: A prevalence study. *Psicologia, Reflexão e Crítica, 27*(4), 759-767. doi: http://dx.doi.org/10.1590/1678-7153.2014274167

dosReis, S., Barksdale, C. L., Sherman, A., Maloney, K., & Charach, A. (2010). Stigmatizing experiences of parents of children with a new diagnosis of ADHD. *Psychiatric Services, 61*(8), 811-6.

dosReis, S., Mychailyszyn, M. P., Evans-Lacko, S., Beltran, A., Riley, A. W., & Myers, M. A. (2009). The meaning of attention-deficit/hyperactivity disorder medication and parents' initiation and continuity of treatment for their child. *Journal of Child and Adolescent Psychopharmacology, 19*(4), 377-83. doi: http://dx.doi.org/10.1089/cap.2008.0118

dosReis, S., Mychailyszyn, M. P., Myers, M., & Riley, A. W. (2007). Coming to terms with ADHD: How urban African-American families come to seek care for their children. *Psychiatric Services, 58*(5), 636-41.

Douglas, V. I. (1972). Stop, look and listen: The problem of sustained attention and impulse control in hyperactive and normal children. *Canadian Journal of Behavioural Science/Revue Canadienne Des Sciences Du Comportement, 4*(4), 259-282. doi:10.1037/h0082313

Doyle, A. E., Biederman, J., Seidman, L. J., Weber, W., & Faraone, S. V. (2000). Diagnostic efficiency of neuropsychological test scores for discriminating boys with and without attention deficit–hyperactivity disorder. *Journal of Consulting and Clinical Psychology, 68*(3), 477-488. doi:10.1037/0022-006X.68.3.477

Dreyer, S. A., O'Laughlin, L., Moore, J., & Milam, Z. (2010). Parental adherence to clinical recommendations in an ADHD evaluation clinic. *Journal of Clinical Psychology, 66*(10), 1101-1120. doi:10.1002/jclp.20718

DuPaul, G. J., & Jimerson, S. R. (2014). Assessing, understanding, and supporting students with ADHD at school: Contemporary science, practice, and policy. *School Psychology Quarterly, 29*(4), 379-384. doi:10.1037/spq0000104

Efron, D., Sciberras, E., & Hassell, P. (2008). Are schools meeting the needs of students with ADHD? *Australasian Journal of Special Education, 32*(2), 187-198. doi:10.1080/10300110802047459

Eiraldi, R. B., Mazzuca, L. B., Clarke, A. T., & Power, T. J. (2006). Service utilization among ethnic minority children with ADHD: A model of help-seeking behavior. *Administration and Policy in Mental Health and Mental Health Services Research, 33*(5), 607-22. doi:10.1007/s10488-006-0063-1

Fabiano, G. A. (2007). Father participation in behavioral parent training for ADHD: Review and recommendations for increasing inclusion and engagement. *Journal of Family Psychology, 21*(4), 683-693. doi:10.1037/0893-3200.21.4.683

Fabiano, G. A., Pelham, W. E., Jr., Coles, E. K., Gnagy, E. M., Chronis-Tuscano, A., & O'Connor, B. C. (2009). A meta-analysis of behavioral treatments for attention deficit/hyperactivity disorder. *Clinical Psychology Review, 29*, 129–140. doi:10.1016/j.cpr.2008.11.001

Fabrega, H. (1990). Psychiatric stigma in the classical and medieval period: a review of the literature. *Comprehensive Psychiatry, 31*(4), 289-306.

Fantuzzo, J., Tighe, E., & Childs, S. (2000). Family involvement questionnaire: A multivariate assessment of family participation in early childhood education. *Journal of Educational Psychology, 92*, 367–376. doi:10.1037/0022-0663.92.2.367

Fegert, J., Slawik, L., Wermelskirchen, D., Nübling, M., & Mühlbacher, A. (2011). Assessment of parents' preferences for the treatment of school-age children with ADHD: A discrete choice experiment. *Expert Review of Pharmacoeconomics & Outcomes Res. 11*(3), 245–252 (2011)

Goldman, L. S., Genel, M., Bezman, R. J., & Slanetz, P. J. (1998). Diagnosis and treatment of attention-deficit/hyperactivity disorder in children and adolescents. JAMA: *Journal of the American Medical Association, 279*(14), 1100-1107. doi:10.1001/jama.279.14.1100

Hamrin, V., McCarthy, E. M., B.A., & Tyson, V. (2010). Pediatric psychotropic medication initiation and adherence: A literature review based on social exchange theory. *Journal of Child and Adolescent Psychiatric Nursing, 23*(3), 151-72.

Harvey, E. A., Breaux, R. P., & Lugo-Candelas, C. I. (2016). Early development of comorbidity between symptoms of attention-deficit/hyperactivity disorder (ADHD) and oppositional defiant disorder (ODD). *Journal of Abnormal Psychology, 125*(2), 154-167. doi:10.1037/abn0000090

Hathaway, W. L., & Barkley, R. A. (2003). Self-Regulation, ADHD, & child religiousness. *Journal of Psychology & Christianity, 22*(2), 101.

Hervey-Jumper, H., Douyon, K., & Franco, K. N. (2006). Deficits in diagnosis, treatment and continuity of care in African-American children and adolescents with ADHD. *Journal of the National Medical Association, 98*(2), 233-8.

Johnston, C. C., Seipp, C. C., Hommersen, P. P., Hoza, B. B., & Fine, S. S. (2005). Treatment choices and experiences in attention deficit and hyperactivity disorder: relations to parents' beliefs and attributions. *Child: Care, Health & Development, 31*(6), 669-677. doi:10.1111/j.1365-2214.2005.00555.x

Johnston, C., Mah, J. W., & Regambal, M. (2010). Parenting cognitions and treatment beliefs as predictors of experience using behavioral parenting strategies in families of children with attention-deficit/hyperactivity disorder. *Behavior Therapy, 41*(4), 491-504.

Kaufmann, L., & Nuerk, H. (2008). Basic number processing deficits in ADHD: A broad examination of elementary and complex number processing skills in 9- to 12-year-old children with ADHD-C. *Developmental Science, 11*(5), 692-699.

Kazantzis, N., Deane, F. P., & Ronan, K. R. (2000). Homework assignments in cognitive and behavioral therapy: A meta-analysis. *Clinical Psychology: Science and Practice, 7*, 189–202.

Lietz, C. A. & Zayas, L. E. (2010). Evaluating qualitative research for social work practitioners. *Advances in Social Work, 11*(2):188-202.

Litner, B., & Mann-Feder, V. (2009). Fostering resilience in youth with ADHD. *Relational Child & Youth Care Practice, 22*(3), 35-39.

Maki, K. E., Floyd, R. G., & Roberson, T. (2015). State learning disability eligibility criteria: A comprehensive review. *School*

Psychology Quarterly, 30(4), 457.doi:10.1037/spq0000109

Maniadaki, K. K., Sonuga-Barke, E. E., Kakouros, E. E., &
Karaba, R. R. (2007). Parental beliefs about the nature of
ADHD behaviours and their relationship to referral intentions
in preschool children. *Child: Care, Health & Development,
33*(2), 188-195. doi:10.1111/j.1365-2214.2006.00642.x

Marshall, M. N. (1996). Sampling for qualitative research. *Family
Practice, 13*(6), 522-526.

Martinussen, R., & Major, A. (2011). Working memory
weaknesses in students with ADHD: Implications for
instruction. *Theory into Practice, 50*(1), 68-75.
doi:10.1080/00405841.2011.534943

Mash, E. J., & Barkley, R. A. (2007). *Assessment of Childhood
Disorders* (4th ed.). New York, NY: The Guildford Press.

Mason, M. (2010). Sample size and saturation in PhD studies
using qualitative interviews. *In Forum Qualitative
Sozialforschung/Forum: Qualitative Social Research
11*(3). Retrieved
from http://www.qualitativeresearch.net/index.php/fqs/article/
view/1428/3028

McInnes, A., Humphries, T, Hogg-Johnson, S., & C Tannock, R.
(2003). Listening comprehension and working memory are
impaired in attention-deficit hyperactivity disorder
irrespective of language impairment. *Journal of Abnormal
Child Psychology, 31,* 427443.

Mills, I. (2011). Understanding parent decision making for
treatment of ADHD. *School Social Work Journal, 36*(1), 41-
60.

Moen, Ø. L., Hall-Lord, M. L., & Hedelin, B. (2011). Contending
and adapting every day Norwegian parents' lived experience
of having a child with ADHD. *Journal of Family Nursing,
17*(4), 441-462.

Morton, R. L., Tong, A., Howard, K., Snelling, P., & Webster, A.
C. (2010). The views of patients and carers in treatment
decision making for chronic kidney disease: systematic
review and thematic synthesis of qualitative studies. *BmJ,
340,* c112.2.

Mueller, A. K., Fuermaier, A. B., Koerts, J., & Tucha, L. (2012).
Stigma in attention deficit hyperactivity disorder. *ADHD
Attention Deficit and Hyperactivity Disorders, 4*(3), 101-114.

Mychailyszyn, M. P., dosReis, S., & Myers, M. (2008). African
American caretakers' views of ADHD and use of outpatient
mental health care services for children. *Families, Systems,*

& Health, 26(4), 447-458. doi:10.1037/1091-7527.26.4.447

Olaniyan, O., dosReis, S., Garriett, V., Mychailyszyn, M. P., B.A., Anixt, J., Rowe, P. C., M.D., & Cheng, Tina L,M.D., M.P.H. (2007). Community perspectives of childhood behavioral problems and ADHD among African American parents. *Ambulatory Pediatrics, 7*(3), 226-31.

Owens, J. S., Murphy, C. E., Richerson, L., Girio, E. L.,&Himawan, L. K. (2008). Science to practice in underserved communities: The effectiveness of school mental health programming. *Journal of Clinical Child and Adolescent Psychology, 37,* 434–447. doi:10.1080/15374410801955912

Patton, M. Q. (2002). *Qualitative research and evaluation methods* (3rd ed.). Thousand Oaks, CA: Sage Publications.

Pelham, W. E., Lang, A. R., Atkeson, B., Murphy, D. A., Gnagy, E. M., Greiner, A. R., et al. (1997). Effects of deviant child behavior on parental distress and alcohol consumption in laboratory interactions. *Journal of Abnormal Child Psychology, 25,* 413–424.

Pelham, W. E., Lang, A. R., Atkeson, B., Murphy, D. A., Gnagy, E. M., Greiner, A. R., et al. (1998). Effects of deviant child behavior on parental alcohol consumption. *The American Journal on Addictions, 7,* 103–114.

Pellow, J., Solomon, E., Barnard, C. (2011). Complementary and alternative medical therapies for children with attention-deficit/hyperactivity disorder (ADHD). *Alternative Medicine Review, 16*(4), 323-337.

Peters, K., & Jackson, D. (2009). Mothers' experiences of parenting a child with attention deficit hyperactivity disorder. *Journal of Advanced Nursing, 65*(1), 62-71. doi:10.1111/j.1365-2648.2008.04853.x

Pfiffner, L. J., Mikami, A. Y., Huang-Pollock, C., Easterlin, B., Zalecki, C., & McBurnett, K. (2007). A randomized, controlled trial of integrated home-school behavioral treatment for ADHD, predominantly inattentive type. *Journal of the American Academy of Child & Adolescent Psychiatry, 46,* 1041–1050. doi:10.1097/chi.0b013e318064675f

Pham, A. V., Carlson, J. S., & Kosciulek, J. F. (2009). Ethnic difference in parental beliefs of attention-deficit/hyperactivity disorder and treatment. *Journal of Attention Disorders 13*(6). 584- 591. doi:10.1177/1087054709332391

Power, T. J., Mautone, J. A., Soffer, S. L., Clarke, A. T., Marshall, S. A., Sharman, J., ... & Jawad, A. F. (2012). A family–school intervention for children with ADHD: Results of a randomized clinical trial. *Journal of Consulting and Clinical Psychology, 80*(4), 611.

Rowley, J. (2002). Using case studies in research. *Management Research News, 25*(1), 16-27. Retrieved from http://www.arfasia. org/resources/using_case_study_in_research.pdf

Sayal, K., Ford, T., & Goodman, R. (2010). Trends in recognition of and service use for attention-deficit hyperactivity disorder in Britain, 1999-2004. *Psychiatric Services, 61*(8), 803-10.

Sayal, K., Taylor, E., Beecham, J., & Byrne, P. (2002). Pathways to care in children at risk of attention-deficit hyperactivity disorder. *The British Journal of Psychiatry, 181*(1), 43-48.

Schmitz, M. F., Filippone, P., & Edelman, E. M. (2003). Social representations of attention deficit/hyperactivity disorder, 1988–1997. *Culture & Psychology, 9*(4), 383-406.

Schmitz, M., & Velez, M. (2003). Latino cultural differences in maternal assessments of attention deficit/hyperactivity symptoms in children. *Hispanic Journal of Behavioral Sciences. 25*(1), 110-122. doi:10.1177/0739986303251700

Semrud-Clikeman, M., Walkowiak, J., Wilkinson, A., & Butcher, B. (2010). Executive functioning in children with Asperger syndrome, ADHD-combined type, ADHD-predominately inattentive type, and controls. *Journal of Autism and Developmental Disorders, 40*(8), 1017-1027.

Shallice, T., Marzocchi, G., Coser, S., Del Savio, M., Meuter, R. F., & Rumiati, R. I. (2002). Executive function profile of children with attention deficit hyperactivity disorder. *Developmental Neuropsychology, 21*(1), 43-71. doi:10.1207/S15326942DN2101_3

Sonuga-Barke, E. J. S., Daley, D., & Thompson, M. (2002). Does maternal ADHD reduce the effectiveness of parent training for preschool children's ADHD? *Journal of the American Academy of Child and Adolescent Psychiatry, 41*, 696–702.

Stroh, J., Frankenberger, W., Cornell-Swanson, L., Wood, C., & Pahl, S. (2008). The Use of stimulant medication and behavioral interventions for the treatment of attention deficit hyperactivity disorder: A survey of parents' knowledge, attitudes, and experiences. *Journal of Child and Family Studies, 17*(3), 385-401.

Taylor, M., O'Donoghue, T., & Houghton, S. (2006). To medicate or not to medicate? The decision-making process of Western Australian parents following their child's diagnosis with an attention deficit hyperactivity disorder. International *Journal of Disability, Development & Education, 53*(1), 111-128.

Wallace, N. (2005). The perceptions of mothers of sons with ADHD. *Australian & New Zealand Journal of Family Therapy, 26*(4), 193-199.

Weyandt, L. L., Fulton, K. M., Schepman, S. B., Verdi, G. R., & Wilson, K. G. (2009). Assessment of teacher and school psychologist knowledge of attention-deficit/hyperactivity disorder. *Psychology in the Schools, 46*(10), 951-961.

Yin, R. K. (2009). *Case study research: Design and methods* (4th ed.). Thousand Oaks, CA: Sage Publications.

INDEX

CURRICULUM VITAE

Tenise M. Wall
Ph.D., LMSW, CASAC-T
Middletown, New York
drwall2016@yahoo.com

TEACHING PHILOSOPHY

*My teaching philosophy has been shaped by 11 years
of working in the field of education as a school social worker,
providing trainings to education and mental health staff, and
continuing to expand my own professional knowledge over
the years. My primary focus as an educator is to impart
knowledge, provide an atmosphere conducive to learning,
and to connect students to the joy of being a lifelong learner. I
have been able to accomplish this task through differentiated
instruction; understanding that people acquire and retain
information in a variety of ways. My teaching accommodates
the tactile, task oriented, auditory, and visual learner.
Students have often provided feedback of their appreciation
of the incorporation of real life cases in training and
conference sessions.*

*When designing a curriculum and instructional
planning the objective is clearly identified and all content
works to support that objective. There are many assessments
that can be used to assess student learning and I support
using a variety of methods beyond traditional tests/exams to
allow students to demonstrate their understanding of a
particular subject area. As I follow these tenets of teaching it
has increased my passion for the art of instruction. When I
am in the "teacher mode" there is a contagious excitement for
learning that is hard to miss. Faces light up as they are*

pushed to think more critically about the subject at hand, or are learning new information and it is all beginning to connect for them. Having the opportunity to instruct others through trainings, and conferences has fostered the deep love I have for the art of teaching.

TEACHING AND RESEARCH INTERESTS

Psychology, Social Work, Abnormal Psychology, attention deficit hyperactivity disorder, disruptive behavior, conduct, and oppositional defiance behavior disorder, mental health across the lifespan.

CONSULTING

2008 – current, Consultant/Executive Director
Wall Professional Services, Middletown, New York

- Provide professional speaker's resources within educational environments for professional development of teachers, administrators, and support staff (Washingtonville School District, Enlarged City School District of Middletown, and YMCA)
- Provide Critical Incident Stress Management (CISM) services to community agencies in need following a death or tragic incident (of teachers, students, or an organization's employees, members, or volunteers)
- Provide consultation services to parents and caregivers in need of direction in the treatment and obtaining access to academic, behavior, and mental health resources, and understanding 504 Accommodations as it pertains to their child diagnosed with Attention Deficit Hyperactivity Disorder (ADHD)
- Provide professional speaker's resources to local, national, and international organizations on the topic of ADHD, conduct disorders, and mental illness in children/adolescents and adults (school districts, mental health organizations, colleges, universities, parents, and organizations who work with children and adolescents)

PROFESSIONAL EXPERIENCE

2015 – current, Mental Health Clinician
The Institute for Family Health, Ellenville, NY

- Work with (~160-240) patients monthly, between ages 5 to 95 years old in a community-based healthcare facility assisting patients with decreasing depression, anxiety, behavior, and/or psychotic symptoms while improving overall mental health stability
- Provide clinical evaluations for patients' mental health issues including suicidal and homicidal ideations, depression, anxiety, bipolar, schizophrenia, and post-traumatic stress disorder (PTSD), to attention deficit hyperactivity disorder (ADHD), oppositional defiant disorder (ODD), and Conduct Disorders
- Assess patients; provides clinical diagnosis using the DSM-5; formulate Treatment Plan; conduct reports via rules / regulations in Article 28 facility
- Promoted to Project Leader in the Continued Quality Improvement (CQI) initiative in developing practice and organizational protocols for assessing, diagnosing, and treating ADHD.
- Works as the in-house expert on ADHD whereas all children who present with such diagnosis are referred to.
- Provides substance abuse counseling and conducts intakes for patient consideration in our on-site suboxone treatment program.
- Engages in various evidenced-based treatment modalities to consist of Cognitive Behavior Therapy, Dialectical Behavior Therapy, Problem Solving Therapy, and Motivational Interviewing, as determined by the patient's presenting issues.

2004 – 2015, School Social Worker (K-5)
City School District, Middletown, NY

- Provided counseling services for students/groups; responded to daily crisis intervention / overall behavioral / mental health needs of students
- Performed assessment of suicidal risk / threat to others,

contact with Mobile Mental Health, Orange Regional Medical Center, patient's psychiatrists, counselors, and pediatricians; facilitate Response to Intervention meetings for crisis intervention

- Union representative on District-wide RtI Steering Committee (seven years) for Special Education Review panel member to review files for school compliance with Functional Behavior Assessments & Behavior Intervention Plan's

- Collaborated with outside providers and collaterals: Child Protective Services, Department of Social Services, Preventive Intake Services of Orange County, Network, Orange County Systems of Care, Middletown Police Dept., Orange County Youth Bureau, Big Brothers/Big Sisters, Middletown Cares, Girl Scouts, Boy Scouts of America, and Thrall Library

- Liaison between school and Intensive Day Treatment, Supplemental Program for At-Risk Children, Board of Cooperative Educational Services, and home instruction

- Conduct home visits assessing & providing support to families in need

- Team member on the 504 Accommodation, Committee on Special Education, Attendance, Literacy, School Improvement, and Building Response Teams. Consult with teachers, classroom observations, and key coordinator of Functional Behavioral Assessments (FBA) and Behavior Intervention Plans (BIP)

- Developed and/or implemented more than two dozen programs including: Everyone Matters Week, Peace Builders of the Month Awards assembly, Peace Patrol, TV Turn off Week, Thanksgiving Food Drive, "Souper Bowl Month," Operation Check it Out, Adopt-a-Family Program, Book It Program, Hygiene Drive and No Kid Hungry.

- Developed / implemented The Character Word of the month which the district later used to satisfy their No Child Left Behind Federal requirement for teaching character education

- Provide classroom guidance lessons supporting the Character Word of the Month, anti-bullying lessons, and topics specific to the students' needs

2008 – 2013, Private Practitioner
Wall Professional Services
Newburgh/Middletown, NY

- Provided counseling services to children, adolescents, individuals, and family systems, presenting issues from adjustment issues, behavioral / mood disorders, suicidality, self-injurious behavior, and substance abuse.
- Provided affiliate Employee Assistance Provider (EAP) services; responsible for determining an employee's (staff member) ability to return to work using the CAGE (Cut down, Annoyed, Guilty, and Eye-opener) Assessment for Alcohol Abuse was incorporated via such assessments as related
- Provided psychosocial assessments for substance abuse; designed referrals / treatment plans to reflect supportive services, including outpatient, AA, Al-Anon, Narcotics Anonymous, Mentally Ill Chemically Addicted, Catholic Charities, and community-based programs
- Provided substance abuse counseling in collaboration with community group supports, working with school systems, psychiatrists, substance abuse programs, Behavioral Health Units, collaterals as an affiliate of the PARISH Counseling Network providing faith-based counseling services

2003 – 2011, Inpatient Psychotherapist
Orange Regional Medical Center
Arden Hill Campus, Goshen, NY

- Performed psychosocial assessments on patients assigned to team; daily assessed patients' risks (to self and / or others) within secured facility
- Met with team (daily) to discuss treatment needs of individual patients with diagnoses including: depression, bipolar, borderline personality, schizophrenia, suicidal, homicidal, anxiety, obsessive compulsive, intellectual disability, and substance abuse disorders
- Performed CAGE Assessment for Alcohol Abuse patient assessments as the needs pertained to alcohol; performed more comprehensive substance use/abuse

assessments for patients with substance abuse history
- Facilitated / provided psychotherapy to patients through individual, family, and group sessions. Facilitated weekly MICA (Mentally Ill Chemically Addicted) psychotherapy groups for patients with substance abuse issues simultaneously with mental health needs, including consistent psycho-education about defense mechanisms, triggers identified through people, places, and things, self-care, and benefits of identifying and making SMART goals
- Assessed patients to determine needs for continued inpatient hospitalization; worked within a team modality (with psychiatrist, nurse, and activities therapist); made recommendations for treatment
- Collaborated with outside providers (family members, law enforcement, probation, parole officers, psychiatrists, therapists, medical doctors, Assertive Community Treatment (ACT) Team, Crystal Run Village, Family Homecare agencies, Adult Protective Services (APS), and Child Protective Services) resulting discharge plan to gather the input from all providers involved in the treatment of the patient that assisted in decreasing the patients' likelihood of hospital readmission
- Coordinated discharge services for Mentally Ill Chemically Addicted patients which may include direct transfer to inpatient substance abuse programs such as R.C. Ward, Phelps Memorial, Arms Acres, and more. Assisted in phone Intakes with patients and substance abuse treatment providers

2001 – 2003, Sentencing Advocate
Court Consultation Services, Monroe, NY

- Performed psychosocial assessments for individual clients involved in legal court system
- Interviewed witnesses, spoke to collaterals, reviewed legal documents, and worked closely with attorneys, judges, and the overall court system for clients facing charges of murder, drug possession and sale, violation of probation and parole, sexual assault, driving under the influence of drugs and alcohol, and robbery

- Wrote pre-plea and pre-sentence memorandums and presented to the court upon completion of assessment, background check, and interviews
- Made sentencing recommendations to include the presenting psychosocial, mental health, substance abuse, and other needs of the client to be considered by judge and district attorney during trial sentencing phase; recommendations based on severity of crime, background of patient, and following a clinical assessment of their likelihood of recidivism
- Referred clients as needed to substance abuse treatment programs; developed a system within the professional office for building a library of substance abuse treatment services, protocol for Intakes, and distinguishing between care levels, including community meetings, outpatient programs, and inpatient programs to include therapeutic treatment communities); referred clients to substance abuse programs (in/out of state)
- Worked with Probation & Parole Officers, to encourage / monitoring substance abuse sponsors for community-based Alcoholics Anonymous (AA), Narcotics Anonymous (NA) meetings
- Coordinated drug screenings with Quest Diagnostics; reviewed findings with lab technicians for reports to court for clients
- Provided supervision services for mandated supervised visitation ordered via Family Court

03/97 – 01/02, Founder/Owner
TC's Tender Touch, Middletown, NY

- Established a licensed home daycare program for children ages 6 weeks – 12 years old, providing the supervision, activities, and meeting the daily needs of all children enrolled in care

FACILITATED TRAININGS/PRESENTATIONS

- 04/16, ADHD: What parents need to know, what it is, and what to do, Washingtonville School District Parent-Teacher Association to 40 district teaching staff,

administrators, and support staff, Washingtonville, NY
- 04/2016, ADHD: School and parents- The great divide and how to bridge the gap, Washingtonville School District Teacher Center, to 30 district teaching staff, administrators and support staff, Washingtonville, NY
- 04/2016, ADHD: School based interventions that work, Washingtonville School District Teacher Center, to 30 district teaching staff, administrators and support staff, Washingtonville, NY
- 04/2016, ADHD & learning disabilities: Understanding executive dysfunction in ADHD, Washingtonville School District Teacher Center, to 30 district teaching staff, administrators and support staff, Washingtonville, NY
- 03/2016, ADHD: What is it all about? Etiology, prevalence, and current trends, Washingtonville School District Teacher Center, to 30 district teaching staff, administrators and support staff, Washingtonville, NY
- 2014, Working with challenging behaviors: From understanding to interventions that work, to approximately 100 regional staff of the YMCA over 2 sessions, Middletown, NY
- 2014 -03/2016, An overview of oppositional defiant disorder with school setting applications, Middletown School District Teacher Center & Washingtonville School District Teacher Center, to approximately 150 district teaching staff, administrators and support staff over 3 sessions, Middletown, New York & Washingtonville, NY
- 2010, Diversity beyond poverty. Middletown School District Teacher Center, to 100 district teaching staff, administrators and support staff over 2 sessions, Middletown, NY
- 2010, Peace Builders Trainer in Service, to 75 attendees, Middletown, NY
- 2014, Understanding the Role of a School Social Worker, Truman Moon Parent- Teacher Organization, to 25 parents, Middletown, NY
- 2009/2010, Deconstructing the complexities of diversity. Middletown School District Teacher Center, to ~200 teaching staff, administrators, and support staff, over four sessions, Middletown, NY

EDUCATION

05/16, Doctorate of Philosophy, General Psychology, Capella University, Harold Abel School of Social and Behavioral Sciences, Minneapolis, MN; Dissertation topic: "The experience of parents seeking treatment for their child who is diagnosed with ADHD." GPA: 3.93 Graduation with Distinction.

08/03, Master of Social Work, Clinical Social Work and Crisis Intervention, Graduate School of Social Service, Fordham University, Tarrytown, NY

08/02, Bachelor of Science, Marist College School of Behavioral and Social Science, Goshen, NY

08/01, Associates of Arts, Liberal Arts Degree. Orange County Community College, Middletown, NY

LICENSURE

- 12/15, Certified Alcohol and Substance Abuse Counselor-T – Alcohol & Drug Abuse Council, Office of Alcoholism and Substance Abuse Services, Albany, NY
- 09/08, School Social Worker – State of New York Department of Education Office of Professions/ Permanent School Social Worker Certificate, Albany, New York
- 09/04, Licensed Master Social Worker (LMSW) – State of New York Department of Education Office of Professions, Albany, New York

CERTIFICATIONS RECEIVED

- 2016, Certified Rape Crisis Counselor, Ulster County Probation & Crime Victim's Assistance Program, Kingston, NY
- 2016, Certificate, Problem Solving Therapy, Institute for Family Health, New York, NY
- 2016, Board Certified Christian Counselor, International

Board of Christian Counselors, Forest, VA
- 2015, Certified in Children & Adolescent Crisis Response in School Settings, International Critical Incident Stress Foundation (ICISF), Baltimore, NY
- 2012, Certified Question, Persuade, Refer (QPR) Suicide Prevention Gatekeeper Instructor, QPR For Suicide Prevention, New Hampton, NY
- 2012, Certificate of Completion in the Marriage Mentors Program, American Association of Christian Counselors, Forest, VA
- 2012, Certificate of Completion for Dignity Act Coordinator, The New York State Center for School Safety, Goshen, NY
- 2011, Certified Supervisor in Field Instruction (SIFI)-Fordham University, Harrison, NY
- 2010, Fordham University training certificate "The Fordham Center for Non-Profit Leader Program," New York, NY
- 2010, Certified to administer the Child & Adolescent Needs Assessment Tools for Schools—CANS, The Praed Foundation and The University of Ottawa, Goshen, NY
- 2009, Certified Professional Life Coach, Light University - American Association of Christian Counselors, Forest, VA
- 2008, Certified NYS Court Evaluator – Article 81 Incapacity Hearings, Sadin Institute on Law & Public Policy, Brookdale Center for Healthy Aging & Longevity of Hunter College, New York, NY
- 2008 – 2016, Board Certified Professional Christian Counselor, American Association of Christian Counselors, Forest, VA
- 2006, Certified in Aggression Replacement Therapy, Orange County Youth Bureau, Goshen, NY

SPECIALIZED TRAININGS COMPLETED

- 2016, Understanding ADHD in Adults, National Association for Continuing Education
- 2016, Understanding ADHD in Adults
- 2016, Treatment that Works: Learning to Effectively Use the Unified Protocols for Trans-Diagnostic Treatment of

Emotional Disorders, Trauma Institute of Orange County, Goshen, NY
- 2016, Safety Planning Intervention for Suicide Prevention, Center for Practice Innovations at Columbia Psychiatry New York State Psychiatric Institute
- 2016, Safety Planning Intervention for Suicide Prevention, Center for Practice Innovations at Columbia Psychiatry New York State Psychiatric Institute
- 2016, Psychosocial Interventions for ADHD in Adults, National Association for Continuing Education
- 2016, Problem Solving Treatment in Primary Care 12 Hours Group Supervision, Institute for Family Health, New York, NY
- 2016, Problem Solving Treatment for Primary Care, Institute for Family Health, Kingston, NY
- 2016, Pharmacotherapy of Adults and Co-Morbid Conditions, National Association for Continuing Education
- 2016, Pharmacotherapy of Adults and Co-Morbid Conditions, National Association for Continuing Education
- 2016, One Love Foundation- Escalation Screening, Mid-Hudson Substance Abuse Prevention, Fishkill, NY
- 2016 Module 39: Co-Occurring Disorders in Adolescents, Center for Practice Innovations at Columbia Psychiatry New York State Psychiatric Institute
- 2016 Module 32: Clinical Leadership, Center for Practice Innovations at Columbia Psychiatry New York State Psychiatric Institute
- 2016 Module 30 & 31: Clinical Supervision I & II, Center for Practice Innovations at Columbia Psychiatry New York State Psychiatric Institute
- 2016 Module 29: Integrating Medical, Psychiatric and Addiction Treatment Services, Center for Practice Innovations at Columbia Psychiatry New York State Psychiatric Institute
- 2016 Module 27: Understanding the Use of Medications for Clients with COD, Center for Practice Innovations at Columbia Psychiatry New York State Psychiatric Institute
- 2016 Module 26: Achieving Recovery in the Real World, Center for Practice Innovations at Columbia Psychiatry New York State Psychiatric Institute

- 2016 Module 25: Taking Responsibility for Your Recovery, Center for Practice Innovations at Columbia Psychiatry New York State Psychiatric Institute
- 2016 Module 24: Philosophy and Perspectives of Recovery, Center for Practice Innovations at Columbia Psychiatry New York State Psychiatric Institute
- 2016 Module 23: Work with Families and Other Close Supporters, Center for Practice Innovations at Columbia Psychiatry New York State Psychiatric Institute
- 2016 Module 22: Individual Interventions, Center for Practice Innovations at Columbia Psychiatry New York State Psychiatric Institute
- 2016 Module 21: Social Skills Training, Center for Practice Innovations at Columbia Psychiatry New York State Psychiatric Institute
- 2016 Module 20: CBT for Treating Anxiety, Depression, and Trauma-Related Problems, Center for Practice Innovations at Columbia Psychiatry New York State Psychiatric Institute
- 2016 Module 19: CBT for Coping Skills and Problem Solving, Center for Practice Innovations at Columbia Psychiatry New York State Psychiatric Institute
- 2016, Module 18: Peer Recovery Supports in the Community, Center for Practice Innovations at Columbia Psychiatry New York State Psychiatric Institute
- 2016, Module 17: Active Treatment/Relapse Groups, Center for Practice Innovations at Columbia Psychiatry New York State Psychiatric Institute
- 2016, Module 11: Motivational Interviewing and Harm Reduction, Center for Practice Innovations at Columbia Psychiatry New York State Psychiatric Institute
- 2016, Module 10: Motivational Interviewing III, Center for Practice Innovations at Columbia Psychiatry New York State Psychiatric Institute
- 2016, Module 02: Implementing Co-Occurring Disorders (COD) Treatment, Center for Practice Innovations at Columbia Psychiatry New York State Psychiatric Institute
- 2016, Managing ADHD Medications in Outpatient Settings: A Guide for Primary Care Providers, National Association for Continuing Education

- 2016, Maintenance and Follow-up Care for Adults with ADHD, National Association for Continuing Education
- 2016, Improving Executive Function in Adult ADHD, National Association for Continuing Education
- 2016, Highlights from the partnership for Success Coalition, Mid-Hudson Substance Abuse Prevention, Fishkill, NY
- 2016, Insights into the Use/Misuse of Opiates and Synthetic Marijuana, Mid-Hudson Substance Abuse Prevention, Fishkill, NY
- 2016, Intranasal NARCAN Training, Mid-Hudson Substance Abuse Prevention, Fishkill, NY
- 2016, Get the 4-1-1: Everything Primary Care Providers Should Know About Parent Training in Behavior Therapy While Working with Families with Young Children with ADHD, Charlotte Area Health Education Center
- 2016, Beyond Transference, Counter Transference and Emerging Neuroscience: Using Yourself to Help Client's Recovery and Healing, Orange County Department of Mental Health, Montgomery, NY
- 2016, Assessment of Adult ADHD, National Association for Continuing Education
- 2016, Assessing Functional Outcomes in Young Adults with ADHD, National Association for Continuing Education
- 2016, Assessing and Managing Suicide Risk: Core Competencies for Mental Health Professionals, Suicide Prevention Resource Center, New York, NY
- 2016, ADHD in Adults: Making the Diagnosis and Optimizing Treatment, National Association for Continuing Education
- 2016, ADHD in Adults- Differential and Coexisting Diagnosis, National Association for Continuing Education
- 2016, Cognitive Processing Therapy course, Medical University of South Carolina Department of Psychiatry and Behavioral Sciences (9-hours)
- 2016, 6th Annual Conference Trauma in the 21st Century, Trauma Institute of Orange County, Middletown, NY
- 2016 2-Day Integrating Playful TFCBT into the Treatment of Traumatized Children, Mid-Atlantic Play Therapy

Institute, Arlington, VA
- 2015, To Refer or Not to Refer, Duchess County BOCES, Beacon, NY
- 2015, The Art and Craft of Motivation, NYSUT Education & Learning Trust, Middletown, NY
- 2015, Structuring Therapy for Success, Trauma Institute of Orange County, Goshen, NY
- 2015, Stop the Cycle: Strategies to Help with Avoidance/Escape Behaviors in Those with PTSD, Trauma Institute of Orange County, Goshen, NY
- 2015, Reasoning with Unreasonable People: Focus on Disorders of Emotional Regulation, Institute for Brain Potential, Poughkeepsie, NY
- 2015, Poverty and the Impact on Learning: Using Strategies to Narrow the Achievement Gap, Middletown Teacher Center, Middletown, NY
- 2015 Module 28: Generating the Collaborative Treatment Plan, Center for Practice Innovations at Columbia Psychiatry New York State Psychiatric Institute
- 2015, Module 16: Persuasion Groups, Center for Practice Innovations at Columbia Psychiatry New York State Psychiatric Institute
- 2015, Module 14: Later Stages of Change, Center for Practice Innovations at Columbia Psychiatry New York State Psychiatric Institute
- 2015, Module 13: Early Stages of Change, Center for Practice Innovations at Columbia Psychiatry New York State Psychiatric Institute
- 2015, Module 12: Stage-Wise Treatment, Center for Practice Innovations at Columbia Psychiatry New York State Psychiatric Institute
- 2015, Module 08 & 9: Motivational Interviewing I & II, Center for Practice Innovations at Columbia Psychiatry New York State Psychiatric Institute
- 2015, Module 07: Differentiating Substance Use and Psychiatric Symptoms, Center for Practice Innovations at Columbia Psychiatry New York State Psychiatric Institute
- 2015, Module 06: Assessment of Psychiatric Disorders, Center for Practice Innovations at Columbia Psychiatry New York State Psychiatric Institute

- 2015, Module 05: Assessment of Substance Use Disorder, Center for Practice Innovations at Columbia Psychiatry New York State Psychiatric Institute
- 2015, Module 04: Screening for Psychiatric Disorders, Center for Practice Innovations at Columbia Psychiatry New York State Psychiatric Institute
- 2015, Module 03: Screening for Substance Use, Center for Practice Innovations at Columbia Psychiatry New York State Psychiatric Institute
- 2015, Module 01: Introduction, Center for Practice Innovations at Columbia Psychiatry New York State Psychiatric Institute
- 2015, Improving Executive Function: Assessment & Interventions for Better Thinking, Self-Regulation & Academic Success in Children & Adolescents, PESI Behavioral Healthcare, Poughkeepsie, NY
- 2015, Connecting the Continuum: Emerging Drug Trends, Substance Use Disorders and Advances in Recovery, The Center for Prevention and Counseling School of Health and Addiction Studies, Hamburg, NJ
- 2015, Assessment of Suicidal Risk Using C-SSRS, Center for Practice Innovations at Columbia Psychiatry New York State Psychiatric Institute
- 2015, An Introduction to Doing Therapy with Sexually Abused Children & Teens, Trauma Institute of Orange County, Goshen, NY
- 2015, 2nd Annual Mid-Hudson Substance Abuse Prevention Conference, New York State Office of Alcoholism and Substance Abuse Services, Fishkill, NY
- 2014, Guardianship Training, Sadin Institute on Law & Public Policy, Brookdale Center for Healthy Aging & Longevity of Hunter College, New York, NY
- 2014, Understanding, Assessing and Treating Childhood Trauma, The Trauma Institute of Orange County, Goshen, NY
- 2014, Treating School Avoidance and Emotional Dysregulation: Using a Neuro-Developmentally Informed Therapeutic Model, A Solution-Focused Therapeutic Approach, Orange County Department of Mental Health, Goshen, NY

- 2014, Executive Dysfunction: Effective Strategies & Interventions for Children & Adolescents, PESI Behavioral Health, Poughkeepsie, NY
- 2014, DSM 5 The Next Generation, National Association of Social Workers, Albany, NY
- 2013, Dr. Kutcher's presentation on ADHD, Enlarged City School District of Middletown, Middletown, NY
- 2013, 10-Hour Training Course for Trauma-Focused Cognitive-Behavioral Therapy, Medical University of South Carolina
- 2012, Wired Differently: Prevention & Interventions for Students with "Acting Out" & "Acting In" Disorders, PESI Behavioral Health, Poughkeepsie, NY
- 2012, The Dignity Act: An Interactive Workshop for the Dignity Act Coordinator (DAC), New York State Center for School Safety, Middletown, NY
- 2011, The Effects of Trauma on Childhood Development, Mental Health Association, Orange County, Goshen, NY
- 2011, Teaching Higher Order Thinking Skills, Middletown Teacher Center, Middletown, NY
- 2011, Strategies to engage ELL's in the Content Areas, Middletown Teacher Center, Middletown, NY
- 2011, Classroom Management Workshop Series, Middletown Teacher Center, Middletown, NY
- 2011, Accelerating Brain Power I & II, Middletown Teacher Center, Middletown, NY
- 2010, What Great Teachers Do Differently by Todd Whitaker, Enlarged City School District of Middletown, Middletown, NY
- 2010, The Use of Play Therapy & Cognitive-Behavioral Skills Building Therapy Approaches with Traumatized Children & Adolescents, Enlarged City School District of Middletown, Middletown, NY
- 2010, The Effects of Trauma on Childhood Development, Enlarged City School District of Middletown, Middletown, NY
- 2010, Teen Suicide Prevention Training, Enlarged City School District of Middletown, Middletown, NY
- 2010, RtI Practical Strategies for Intervening with Students Before They Fall too far Behind in Reading,

Enlarged City School District, Middletown, Middletown, NY

- 2010, Response to Intervention: Intervening with Students in Reading, Bureau of Education & Research, Fishkill, NY
- 2010, Peace Builders Train the Trainer, Peace Partners Inc., Middletown, NY
- 2010, Growing Through Grief, National Board of Certified Counselors
- 2010, 5 Kids in My Class Are Ruining it For Everybody, Enlarged City School District, Middletown, Middletown, NY
- 2009, Temporary Issues Facing Youth from Risk to Resiliency, Middletown, NY
- 2009, NASW Purpose & Possibility Conference, National Association of Social Workers, Albany, NY
- 2009, Introduction to EMDR therapy, National Association of Social Workers, Chester, NY
- 2009, Disability Awareness, Middletown Teacher Center, Middletown, NY
- 2009, Depression: Breaking the Silence in Communities of Color, National Association of Social Workers, New Rochelle, NY
- 2009, A Systematic Approach for working with adolescent boys who have engaged in sexually abusive behavior, National Association of Social Workers, New Hampton, NY
- 2008, Understanding the NASW Code of Ethics, National Association of Social Workers
- 2008, 4 Part series: Discipline is not a Dirty Word, Cornell Cooperative Extension, Middletown, NY
- 2008, Creating a Climate of Success: Students with Disabilities, Enlarged City School District of Middletown, Middletown, NY
- 2008, A Showcase of Services for High Risk Children, Youth & Families in Orange County, Orange County Department of Mental Health, Goshen, NY
- 2008 Power of Social Work Conference, National Association of Social Workers, Albany, NY
- 2008, 2-Day Advanced Dialectical Behavior Therapy Training, Dr. Galietta, Goshen, New York

- 2007, 2-Day Introduction to Dialectical Behavioral Therapy, Dr. Galieta, Goshen, New York
- 2007, Working Effectively with Behavior Disordered Children and Adolescents, CMI Education Institute, Inc., Paramus, NJ
- 2007, Understanding Adolescent Health: The Social Worker's Role, National Association of Social Workers
- 2007, Improving Your IST Team, OUBOCES, Goshen, NY
- 2007, Guidance Expo, Westchester Putnam College Conference, Inc., White Plains, NY
- 2007, Autism Spectrum Disorders, Middletown Teachers Center, Middletown, NY
- 2007, 2-Day Child & Adolescent Violence Workshop, OUBOCES, Suffern, NY
- 2006, Understanding HIV/AID: The Social Worker's Role, National Association of Social Worker
- 2006, How to Handle the Hard to Handle Student, Applebaum Training Institute, Poughkeepsie, NY
- 2005, Understanding the Bipolar Child & Adolescent, and Cutting & Self Injurious Behavior: Why Do It? Mental Health Association of Orange County, Goshen, NY
- 2005, Ethics: Black, White or Gray? National Association of Social Workers, Poughkeepsie, NY
- 2005, 7 Secrets to Managing a Healthier, New York State Office of Alcoholism and Substance Abuse Services, Goshen, NY
- 2004, Training in Identification and Reporting of Child Abuse and Maltreatment, The University of the State of New York, State Education Department, Suffern, NY
- 2004, Creating a Climate for Success, Enlarged City School District of Middletown, Middletown, NY
- 2003, To Heal is to Empower: Addressing Group Oppression in Mental Health and Chemical Dependency, Orange County Department of Mental Health Chemical Dependency Division, Goshen, NY
- 2003, Trauma: Differential Diagnosis and Treatment, Putnam Family and Community Services, Fishkill, NY
- 2003, Trauma and Childhood Mental Disorder Foundations of Dual Disorders: The Basis for Treatment,

Orange County Department of Mental Health, Goshen, NY

- 2003, Psycho-education or Psychotherapy for Dual Disorders? Orange County Department of Mental Health, Goshen, NY
- 2003, Introduction to Psychodrama, Hudson Valley Psychodrama Institute, Goshen, NY
- 2001, Thinking About Curriculum, New York State Office of Children and Family Services, Middletown, NY
- 2001, Ready, Set, Go: Taking Your Program Outside, New York State Office of Children and Family Services, Middletown, NY
- 2001, Meeting the Nutritional Needs of Children in Group Care, New York State Office of Children and Family Services, Middletown, NY
- 2001, Managing Crisis in Your Program, New York State Office of Children and Family Services, Middletown, NY
- 2001, Managing Challenging Behavior, New York State Office of Children and Family Services, Middletown, NY
- 2001, Making a Difference: Quality School-age Care, New York State Office of Children and Family Services, Middletown, NY
- 2001, Integrating Children with Disabilities in Your Program, New York State Office of Children and Family Services, Middletown, NY
- 2001, Creative Activities: How to Structure for Success, New York State Office of Children and Family Services, Middletown, NY
- 2001, Creating a Healthy Child Care Program, New York State Office of Children and Family Services, Middletown, NY
- 2001, Child Abuse and Maltreatment: Identification and Prevention, New York State Office of Children and Family Services, Middletown, NY
- 2000, Play: Your Role in Making it Work, New York State Office of Children and Family Services, Middletown, NY
- 1999, Planning Ahead: Thinking About Curriculum, New York State Office of Children and Family Services, Middletown, NY
- 1999, Nutrition and Health Needs of Infants and Children

& Safety and Security Procedures, New York State Office
of Children and Family Services, Middletown, NY
- 1999, Managing your Childcare Business, New York
State Office of Children and Family Services, Middletown,
NY
- 1999, Child Abuse and Maltreatment Identification and
Prevention, New York State Office of Children and Family
Services, Middletown, NY

Critical Incident Stress Management (CISM), International Critical Incident Stress Foundation Courses Completed

- 2012, Compassion Fatigue Prevention for Crisis
Counselors, Conducting Effective Drills & Simulations in
Schools, International Critical Incident Stress Foundation,
Goshen, NY
- 2010, Overview of all CISM Concepts: Update in the
Standards of Care, International Critical Incident Stress
Foundation, Goshen, NY
- 2009, 14 Hours, Suicide Prevention, Intervention and
Postvention, International Critical Incident Stress
Foundation, Goshen, NY
- 2008, 14 Hours, Responding to School Crises: An
Integrated Multi-Component Crisis Intervention Approach,
International Critical Incident Stress Foundation, Goshen,
NY
- 2008, 14 Hours, From Trauma to Addictions, International
Critical Incident Stress Foundation, Goshen, NY
- 2007, 13 Hours, Critical Incident Stress Management
Application: Individual Crisis Intervention and Peer
Support, International Critical Incident Stress Foundation,
Goshen, NY
- 2005, 14 Hour, Critical Incident Stress Management
Application with Children, International Critical Incident
Stress Foundation, Goshen, NY
- 2004, 14 Hour, Critical Incident Stress Management:
Groups Crisis Intervention, International Critical Incident
Stress Foundation, Goshen, NY
- 2004, 14 Hour, Critical Incident Stress Management:
Advanced Group Crisis Intervention, International Critical
Incident Stress Foundation, Goshen, NY

PUBLICATIONS/ARTICLES/HIGHLIGHTS

Wall, T. (2016). The Experience of Parents in Seeking Treatment for their Child Diagnosed with ADHD. Virginia Beach / Richmond, VA: DBC Publishing.

Wall, T. (2016). *The Experience of Parents Seeking Treatment for their Child who is Diagnosed with* Attention Deficit Hyperactivity Disorder. (Doctoral dissertation). Retrieved from http://search.proquest.com/docview/1803639157

Wall. (2013, Mar.). Letter to the Times Herald Record Editor.

Wall. (2013). National Association of Social Workers Help Starts Here Black History Month. http://www.helpstartshere.org/2013-black-history-month-celebration

Wall, (2011, Aug.). Hudson Valley Parent Magazine On-line blogger. Be Mindful Not to Share "First Day of School" Fears with Your Children.

Wall, (2011, July). Hudson Valley Parent Magazine On-line blogger. Teens Who Text – It's Not All Bad.

Wall. (2011, May). Hudson Valley Parent Magazine On-line blogger. The Importance of Setting Limits.

Wall. (2011, April). Hudson Valley Parent Magazine On-line blogger. Introduction.

Wall. (2009). March is National Professional Social Workers Month. Middletown Teacher Association News, 8.

Wall, T. (2008). Pain to Purpose: Look What Jesus Did. Kearney, NE: Morris Publishing.

Wall. (2003). (Sharing the Journey, Marist College Adult Program 1995 to 2003.

AWARDS AND SPECIAL RECOGNITIONS

- 2016, Graduation with Distinction (3.93 Cumulative GPA), Capella University
- 2015, City of Middletown Certificate of Recognition for Contributions to the Community, Mayor DeStefano
- 2014, Certificate of Successful Participation for Implementing No Kid Hungry within Truman Moon School, Middletown Lion's Club

- 2011, Peace Builder of the Year through the Peace Coach Program, Peace Partners Inc
- 2010, Certificate of Recognition for Service on the Committee for Nominations & Leadership Identification & Commitment to the Advancement of the Mission and Goals of the NASW-NYS Chapter and its Members
- 2009, Tribute to Women of Achievement of Orange County in Education, Girl Scouts Heart of the Hudson, Hudson, NY
- 2009, State of New York Legislative Resolution Commending Tenise Wall upon the Occasion of Her Designation as the 2009 Woman of Achievement in Education by the Girl Scouts Heart of the Hudson and YMCA Orange County, Adopted in Senate on April 21, 2009 by Senators Bonacic, Larkin, and Morahan. Senate No. 1345.
- 2009, Recognition for Outstanding Dedication and Achievement in Her Respective Profession and Field, US Senator Charles E. Schumer
- 2009, Orange County Executive Certificate of Recognition on Being Honored by Tribute of Women of Achievement of Orange County, Edward Diana, County Executive
- 2009, Orange County Clerk Certificate of Recognition for Women of Achievement Award in Education, Donna Benson, County Clerk
- 2009, NYS Assembly Certificate of Merit for Tribute to Women of Achievement of Orange County, Annie Rabbit, Member of Assembly
- 2009, New York State Assembly Certificate of Merit, Nancy Calhoun, Assembly Member
- 2009, Distinguished Service Award of the County of Orange in Recognition of Exceptional Representation of your Profession, Roxanne Donnery, Chairwoman of The Legislature of Orange County
- 2009, Certificate of Special Congressional Recognition of Outstanding and Invaluable Service to the Community from, Maurice Hinchey, Member of Congress
- 2009, Certificate of Special Congressional Recognition in Outstanding and Invaluable Service to the Community, John Hall, Member of Congress

- 2009, Certificate of Recognition for Outstanding Contributions to the Advancement of the Mission and Goals of the Hudson Valley Division of the NASW-NYS Chapter
- 2009, Certificate of Recognition For Contribution to the NASW-NYS Chapter Leadership Training Institute, National Association of Social Workers.
- 2000 – 2002, Dean's List, four semesters, Marist College
- 2000, Associate of the Quarter, TJ Maxx Middletown, NY
- 1996, Basic Operations, McDonalds Corporation, Bloomfield, NJ

PROFESSIONAL ASSOCIATIONS

- 2016 – Present, Board Certified Christian Counselor: Board of Christian Professional and Pastoral Counselors
- 2012 – Present, International Certified Christian Chaplain: International Federation of Christian Chaplains Inc.
- 2012 – 2013, National Association for the Advancement of Colored People member
- 2010 – Present, International Critical Incident Stress Foundation Inc. member
- 2008 – 2016, Board Certified Professional Christian Counselor: Board of Christian Professional and Pastoral Counselors
- 2008 – 2011, American Association of Christian Counselors member
- 2006 -2013, National Association of Social Workers member
- 2002 – Present, The Gamma Eta Chapter
- 2000 – 2003, Child Care Council of Orange County member

VOLUNTEER EXPERIENCE

- 2016 – Present, Ulster County Crime Victim's Assistance Program
- 2010 – 2013, Participant, Give An Hour
- 2009 – 2010, National Association of Social Workers Committee on Nominations and Leadership Identifications

- 2006 – 2010, National Association of Social Worker Division Member
- 2005 – 2015, Orange County Crisis Team
- 2004 – 2015, Truman Moon PTO member, staff representative
- 2003 – 2004, Monhagen Middle School Executive Board Secretary
- 2002 – 2004, Mental Health Association, Rape Crisis Advocate
- 2002 – 2003, Head Start Parent Volunteer
- 1995 – 1996, Middletown Pre-Kindergarten Program Volunteer

Experience of Parents in Seeking Treatment for
their Child Diagnosed with ADHD

ABOUT THE AUTHOR

Tenise M. Wall, Ph.D. currently works as a psychotherapist providing clinical services to patients with a variety of mental health and behavioral disorders. She worked as a school social worker and personally counseled more than 1000+ children and adolescents during her tenure. She has additional experience in psychiatric, forensic, and community social work. Dr. Wall earned a Doctorate in Psychology and a Masters and Bachelor of Science specializing in social work. She has extensive experience working within the substance abuse field and is a Certified Alcohol and Substance Abuse Counselor –Trainee (CASAC-T).

She was awarded the 2009 Orange County, NY Woman of Achievement Award in the area of Education. She has received certificates of acknowledgement for outstanding service to her community and within her field by the County

*Experience of Parents in Seeking Treatment for
their Child Diagnosed with ADHD*

Executive, Senators, House of Representatives, County Clerk, Assembly Members, Members of Congress, her Mayor, community organizations, and the National Association of Social Workers (NASW). She published her Doctoral dissertation, blogs as a contributing professional blogger for an online magazine, and the book *Pain to Purpose – Look What Jesus Did!*

Dr. Wall is married and has three children with whom she enjoys spending time. One of their favorite family functions is going on vacations to explore other cultures: food, language, and customs. Shopping is always a 'must do' on these occasions. Dr. Wall resides in New York State and spends her time cooking new recipes, trying new restaurants, and now that her doctoral studies are complete, trying her hand at cupcake baking and decorating.

Are you in need of a professional speaker on the subject of ADHD or other mental health issues? Dr. Wall is available for public speaking engagements and can design a program specific to your needs. Contact Dr. Wall for Keynote Speeches, Lectures, Breakout Sessions, workshops, conferences, and educational professional development and Superintendent Conference Days.

If you have enjoyed this book, please consider recommending it on social media or leaving a review on Amazon.com and telling others how the book has benefitted you.

**Web-site: www.drwall2016.com
LinkedIn: www.linkedin.com/in/tenisewall
Facebook: https://www.facebook.com/drwall2016/
E-mail: drwall2016@yahoo.com**

ABOUT THE BOOK

Attention Deficit Hyperactivity Disorder (ADHD) continues to be a prevalent childhood diagnosis, for which parents seek treatment for their children. This book examines the experiences of parents as they seek treatment for their child diagnosed with ADHD.

Results of this study showed persistent, emotional, and psychological challenges parents encounter when faced with school systems and the school systems lack of information, incentives, or care to put 504 Accommodations into place. Many study participants felt the schools' attitudes and lack of information were the most difficult part of their treatment seeking experiences, and reported frustration about not having 504 Accommodations implemented or resources provided. The book provides recommendations that involves providing teachers with comprehensive education on the etiology and evidenced-based, best-practices for working with children with ADHD.

The implications for social change include recommendations for practitioners, schools, and the medical community to increase their understanding of parental treatment seeking experiences, and to address such barriers and enhance treatment services. School systems, parents, teachers, and K-12 curriculum developers should investigate this book for discovering the difficulties, frustrations, and emotional upheaval this additional burden places on parents of ADHD children.

www.ingramcontent.com/pod-product-compliance
Lightning Source LLC
Chambersburg PA
CBHW062154270326
41930CB00009B/1533